# BABY
# NAMES

*The Essential List for Choosing the*
*Perfect Name for Your Baby*

KAREN KAUFMAN ORLOFF

ILLUSTRATED BY KERREN BARBAS

PETER PAUPER PRESS, INC.
WHITE PLAINS, NEW YORK

*To Emily and Max—*
*still two of my favorite baby names!*

Designed by Heather Zschock

Illustrations copyright © 2006 Kerren Barbas

Copyright © 2006
Peter Pauper Press, Inc.
202 Mamaroneck Avenue
White Plains, NY 10601
All rights reserved
ISBN 1-59359-925-0
Printed in Hong Kong
7  6  5  4  3  2  1

Visit us at www.peterpauper.com

# THE LITTLE
# BOOK OF
# BABY
# NAMES

# CONTENTS

*A good name is better than
precious ointment.*

ECCLESIASTES 7:1

# INTRODUCTION

"What's in a name?" mused Juliet. Shakespeare's question continues to be pondered by parents-to-be as they mull over the vast naming options. A name is much more than just a way to differentiate one person from another. Your name is your identity, and as names go in and out of style, they can pigeonhole you into a category—one in which you may or may not want to be.

How many times have we met someone and said, "She doesn't look like a Doris" or "Doesn't he seem more like a Chuck than a Charles?"

Celebrities know the importance of names. In the days of old Hollywood, producers were famous for assigning a new name to a

 budding young actor or actress. Today, many up-and-coming performers are creating new identities for themselves by changing their names. If Caryn Johnson had not changed her name to Whoopi Goldberg, would she be just another face in the crowd? If Cornelius Chase had kept his original first name, instead of changing it to Chevy, would we have thought of him as a fresh new comedian or an old-fashioned fuddy-duddy? Dana Owens certainly knew the impact of a name when she called herself Queen Latifah.

As new parents, we often feel a responsibility to give our baby the "perfect name." So many things come into play as moms- and dads-to-be hash out the choices: There are those names we had our hearts set on when we were kids, standard family names, Mom's maiden name, and traditional religious names. And of course, there are the pointed suggestions of meddling mothers-in-law!

Ultimately, though, it is the parents who should decide on their bundle of joy's identity.

That's where *The Little Book of Baby Names* comes in. Each section, "Girls' Names," "Boys' Names," and "Unisex Names," offers a variety of choices, along with each name's origin, meaning, variations, and popular nicknames.

As this is a "Little" book, we couldn't list every name, so we've offered up the "A-list" of today's most popular names, along with traditional choices and a few unique off-the-beaten-path names.

Happy hunting!

# Girls' Names

*Give me a girl at an impressionable age,*
*and she is mine for life.*

MURIEL SPARK,
FROM *THE PRIME OF MISS JEAN BRODIE*

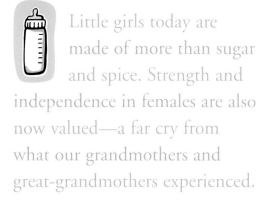

Little girls today are made of more than sugar and spice. Strength and independence in females are also now valued—a far cry from what our grandmothers and great-grandmothers experienced.

Your little girl's name can reflect the age in which she lives. Will she be a free-spirited Fawn, a strong-willed Elizabeth, or a fun-loving Brandi? Here is a selection of wonderful names

for your brand new daughter.

# A

**ABIGAIL** *(Hebrew)* Father's joy
VARIATIONS: Abagael, Abagail, Abagale, Abbigail,
Abbigale, Abbygail, Abbygale
NICKNAMES: Abbey, Abbi, Abbie, Abby, Gael, Gail,
Gale, Gayle

**ADA** *(Latin)* Of noble birth
VARIATIONS: Adda, Aeda, Aida
NICKNAMES: Addie, Addy

**ADORA** *(Latin)* Adored
VARIATIONS: Adoree, Adoria
NICKNAMES: Dora, Dori, Dorie, Dorrie, Dory

**AGNES** *(Greek)* Pure

**AILEEN** *(Irish)* Variant of Helen, meaning
"bright one"

**AISHA** *(Arabic)* Alive
VARIATIONS: Ayeesha, Ayesha

**ALANA** *(Gaelic Irish)* Peaceful, beautiful;
*(Hawaiian)* Offering
VARIATIONS: Alannah, Allanah
NICKNAMES: Allie, Ally, Laney, Lanie, Lany

**ALEXANDRA** *(Greek)* One who defends
VARIATIONS: Alesandra, Alessandra, Alexa,
Alexandria, Alexia, Alexis
NICKNAMES: Alex, Ali, Lexi, Lexie

**ALICE** *(English)* Full of truth
VARIATIONS: Alesha, Alicia, Alisha, Alison, Aliza,
Allison, Alysha, Alyshia, Alysia
NICKNAMES: Ali, Alie

**ALIKA** *(Nigerian)* Beautiful girl
NICKNAME: Ali

**ALISON** *(English)* Variant of Alice, meaning "full
of truth"
VARIATION: Allison
NICKNAMES: Ali, Allie

**AMA** *(Ghanaian)* One born on a Saturday

**AMANDA** *(Latin)* Lovable
VARIATION: Amarinda
NICKNAMES: Manda, Mandi, Mandie, Mandy

**AMARI** *(Hebrew)* Eternal

**AMBER** *(Arabic)* Deep yellow color
VARIATION: Amberlie
NICKNAME: Amby

**AMELIA** *(Latin)* Ambition, work
VARIATIONS: Amalia, Amalie, Emelia
NICKNAMES: Aimee, Amy, Emmy, Millie

**AMY** *(Latin)* Beloved
VARIATIONS: Aimee, Aimie, Amie

**ANASTASIA** *(Greek)* To rise again
VARIATIONS: Anastasie, Anastassia, Anastatia
NICKNAMES: Stacey, Stacy, Tasia

**ANDREA** *(Greek)* Strong, womanly
VARIATIONS: Andra, Andraya, Andriana
NICKNAMES: Andi, Andy

**ANGELA** *(Greek)* Messenger
VARIATIONS: Angel, Angele, Angelica, Angelina,
Angeline, Angelique
NICKNAME: Angie

**ANNA** *(English)* Variant of Hanna, meaning "grace"

**ANNABELLE** *(English)* Combination of Anna
("grace") and Belle ("beautiful")
VARIATION: Anabel

**ANNE** *(English)* Grace
VARIATIONS: Ana, Anita, Ann, Anna, Annabella,
Annabelle, Annette, Annika
NICKNAME: Annie

**ANTOINETTE** *(Latin)* Flourishing

**ARIANA** *(Greek)* Holy
VARIATIONS: Ariane, Arianna, Arianne
NICKNAME: Ari

**ARLENE** *(English)* Vow, pledge
NICKNAME: Lena

**ASHANTI** *(African-American)* Graceful

**ASHLEY** *(English)* Ash tree meadow
VARIATIONS: Ashely, Ashlee, Ashleigh
NICKNAMES: Ash, Lee

**ATHENA** *(Greek)* Goddess of Wisdom
VARIATION: Athene

**AUDREY** *(English)* Strength
VARIATIONS: Aubrey, Audra, Audrie
NICKNAMES: Aud, Audie

**AVA** *(Latin)* Birdlike

**AVERIL** *(English)* Variant of April, symbolizing buds of Spring

# B

**BAINA** *(African)* Sparkling
VARIATION: Bayna

**BAKULA** *(Hindi)* Blossoming plant

**BARBARA** *(Greek)* Strange, foreign
VARIATION: Barbarette
NICKNAMES: Babs, Barb, Barbie, Bobbie

**BEATRICE** *(Latin)* One who brings joy
NICKNAMES: Bea, Trixie

**BELINDA** *(Old Spanish)* Beautiful
VARIATION: Bellalinda
NICKNAMES: Linda, Lindi, Lindy, Lynda, Lynde

**BELLE** *(French)* Beautiful
VARIATIONS: Bela, Bella
NICKNAMES: Bel, Billi, Billie

**BERNICE** *(Greek)* One who brings victory

**BERYL** *(Sanskrit, Arabic, Greek)* Precious jewel
VARIATION: Berylla

**BETH** *(Hebrew)* Worshiper of God
VARIATIONS: Bethanne, Bethany, Bethesda

**BETSY** *(English)* Variant of Elizabeth, meaning "oath of God"

**BEVIN** *(Irish)* Sweet singing maiden
VARIATIONS: Bevan, Beven

**BIANCA** *(Italian)* White
VARIATIONS: Bionca, Bionka, Blanca, Blancha

**BIJOU** *(French)* Jewel

**BILLIE** *(English)* Female form of William, meaning "protector and defender"

**BLYTHE** *(English)* Joyful, happy

**BONITA** *(Spanish)* Pretty
NICKNAME: Bonnie

**BONNIE** *(Scottish)* Pretty, charming

**BRANDY** *(Dutch)* Fiery spirit
VARIATIONS: Brandi, Brandie
NICKNAME: Bran

**BREANNA** *(Celtic)* Strong
VARIATIONS: Breana, Breanne, Brenda, Brenna, Briana, Briane, Briann, Brianna
NICKNAME: Brie

**BRIDGET** *(Irish)* Strength
VARIATIONS: Bridgett, Bridgette, Bridgitte, Brigitte
NICKNAMES: Biddie, Brid, Brit

**BRITTANY** *(English)* From Britain
VARIATIONS: Britany, Britney
NICKNAME: Brit

# C

**CAITLIN** *(Irish)* Pure
VARIATIONS: Caitlyn, Catlin, Kaitlin, Kaitlyn
NICKNAMES: Cat, Katie

**CALIDA** *(Spanish)* Warm and loving

**CALISTA** *(Greek)* Beautiful
VARIATIONS: Calesta, Callista, Kallista
NICKNAMES: Calli, Callie

**CAMILLE** *(French)* Born free
VARIATIONS: Caimile, Camila, Camile, Camilla
NICKNAMES: Cammy, Millie

**1 6**

**CANDACE** *(Greek)* To glow
VARIATIONS: Candase, Candida, Candide
NICKNAMES: Candie, Candy

**CARLA** *(Old Norse)* Female form of Charles, meaning "strong one"
VARIATIONS: Carley, Carly

**CARMEN** *(Latin)* Song

**CAROLINE** *(Latin, French)* Beautiful woman
VARIATIONS: Carlyn, Carol, Carolyn, Karolyn
NICKNAMES: Cara, Carrie, Carry

**CARYS** *(Welsh)* Love

**CASSANDRA** *(Greek)* Prophetess
VARIATIONS: Casandra, Cassandre
NICKNAMES: Cassie, Sandy

**CATAVA** *(African)* Name from a proverb

**CATHERINE** *(Greek)* Pure
VARIATIONS: Catharine, Cathleen, Cathrine, Cathryn, Katarina, Katharine, Katherine, Kathleen, Kathrina, Kathryn, Katrine
NICKNAMES: Cassie, Cat, Cath, Cathee, Cathie, Cathy, Cati, Catie, Caty, Kat, Kate, Kath, Kathy, Kit

**CECILIA** *(Latin)* Blind
VARIATIONS: Cecelia, Cecile, Celisse, Cicely
NICKNAMES: Ces, Cis, Cissy, Sis, Sissy

**CELESTE** *(Latin)* Of the heavens
VARIATIONS: Celesta, Celestia, Celestina
NICKNAME: Celia

**CHANDRA** *(Sanskrit)* Moon

**CHANTAL** *(French)* Singer, song

**CHARLOTTE** *(French)* Little beauty
VARIATIONS: Charla, Charleen, Charlene, Charline, Charlotta, Cheryl, Sheryl
NICKNAMES: Charlie, Lola, Lottie, Totti

**CHELSEA** *(English)* Ship port
VARIATIONS: Chelsa, Chelsee, Chelsey

**CHENOA** *(Native American)* White dove

**CHERYL** *(French)* Variant of Charlotte, meaning "little beauty"
VARIATION: Sheryl

**CHEYENNE** *(Native American)* Name of Native American tribe
VARIATION: Shayanne

**CHLOE** *(Greek)* Fresh-blooming
VARIATION: Cloe
NICKNAME: Clo

**CHRISTINE** *(English)* Anointed one
VARIATIONS: Christa, Christianna, Christie, Christina
NICKNAMES: Chris, Chrissy, Teena, Tina

**CLARA** *(Latin)* Bright
VARIATIONS: Clair, Claire, Clarette, Clarice, Clarisa, Clarissa, Clarisse, Klara

**CLAUDIA** *(Latin)* Lame, limping
VARIATIONS: Claudelle, Claudie, Claudine

**COCO** *(Latin)* Coconut
VARIATION: Koko

**COLETTE** *(French)* Triumphant
VARIATIONS: Collett, Collette, Cosetta, Cosette

**COLLEEN** *(Irish)* Girl

**CONDOLEEZZA** *(American)* With sweetness, based on the Italian "con dolcezza"
NICKNAME: Condi

**CONSTANCE** *(Latin)* Constancy
NICKNAME: Connie

**CORINNE** *(Greek)* Maiden
VARIATIONS: Corinna, Cora

**CORNELIA** *(Latin)* Hornlike
NICKNAMES: Corny, Neely, Nell, Nellie

**COURTNEY** *(English)* Of the court
VARIATIONS: Cortney, Courtenay, Courteney
NICKNAME: Court

**CRYSTAL** *(Latin)* Pure, brilliant

**CYBIL** *(Greek)* Prophet
VARIATIONS: Cybel, Cybill, Sybil

**CYNTHIA** *(Greek)* Moon goddess
NICKNAME: Cindy

**CYRAH** *(African)* Enthroned

# Calendar Girls

*The seasons and months have long
been used as first names for girls.
A few of these, like Autumn
and Summer, are making strong
comebacks. Here are a few more:*

April
Augusta
May
June
Spring
Winter

# D

**DANICA** *(Slavic)* Morning star

**DANIELLE** *(Hebrew, French)* Female form of
Daniel meaning "God is my judge"
VARIATION: Daniele
NICKNAME: Dani

**DAPHNE** *(Greek)* Laurel
VARIATIONS: Dafne, Daphney, Daphny
NICKNAMES: Daff, Daffy

**DARCEY** *(French)* Dark
VARIATIONS: Dara, Darci, Darcie, Daria

**DARLENE** *(English)* Beloved
VARIATIONS: Darla, Darleen, Darline, Daryl

**DAWN** *(German, English)* Daybreak
VARIATION: Dawnn

**DEANDRA** *(African-American)* Newly created name; meaning unknown
VARIATIONS: Deandrea, Deeandra, Diandra, Diandre, Dreandira
NICKNAME: Dee

**DEBORAH** *(Hebrew)* A bee
VARIATIONS: Debora, Deborrah, Debra, Debrah, Devorah
NICKNAMES: Deb, Debbi, Debbie, Debby

**DEIDRE** *(Irish)* Melancholy

**DELIA** *(Greek)* To be seen
VARIATIONS: Dehlia, Della, Delya
NICKNAME: Del

**DELORES** *(Latin)* Sorrowful

**DEMI** *(Latin)* Diminutive of Demetria, Goddess of Fertility
VARIATIONS: Demetra, Dimitra

**DENISE** *(Greek)* Follower of Dionysius, God of wine

**DERICA** *(German)* Beloved leader
VARIATION: Deryca

**DESIREE** *(French)* To long for
VARIATIONS: Desira, Desire, Deziree
NICKNAME: Desi

**DIANA** *(Latin)* Bright one, divine
VARIATIONS: Deana, Deanne, Diane,
Dianne, Dinah, Dionne, Dyan
NICKNAMES: Di, Didi

**DIARA** *(African)* A gift
NICKNAME: Di

**DOMINIQUE** *(Latin)* Of the Lord
VARIATIONS: Dominica, Dominika

**DONNA** *(Italian)* Mistress of a household
VARIATIONS: Donelle, Donnalee
NICKNAMES: Donni, Donny

**DOREEN** *(Greek)* Gift
VARIATION: Dora

**DOROTHY** *(Greek)* Gift of God
VARIATIONS: Dorothea, Thea, Theodora
NICKNAMES: Dodie, Doro, Dottie, Dotty

**DULCIE** *(Latin)* Sweet
VARIATIONS: Dulcea, Dulcee, Dulcy

# E

**EBONY** *(African-American)* Dark, durable wood
VARIATIONS: Ebbony, Eboney, Eboni, Ebonie

**EDEN** *(Hebrew)* Pleasure
VARIATIONS: Eadin, Edana, Edenia, Edin, Edina

**EDITH** *(English)* Precious gift

**EILEEN** *(Irish)* Bright
VARIATIONS: Aileen, Ailene, Alene, Ayleen, Ilene

**ELAINE** *(French)* Bright
VARIATIONS: Elana, Elayne, Ellayne
NICKNAMES: E, El

**ELEANOR** *(English)* Mercy
VARIATIONS: Eleanore, Elenora, Elinor, Ellinor
NICKNAMES: El, Eli, Ella, Ellie, Lennie, Nell

**ELECTRA** *(Greek)* Shining One
VARIATION: Elektra

**ELIANA** *(Hebrew)* Answer to God's prayers
VARIATION: Eliane

**ELIZA** *(English)* From Elizabeth, meaning "oath of God"
NICKNAME: Liza

**ELIZABETH** *(Hebrew)* Oath of God
VARIATIONS: Elisabet, Elisabeth, Elise, Elyse, Elyssa, Lisette, Lizabeth, Lizbeth
NICKNAMES: Bess, Bessie, Beth, Betsey, Betsy, Libby, Liz, Lizzie, Lizzy

**ELLA** *(Greek)* Shining light

**ELLEN** *(English)* Light
VARIATIONS: Elan, Elen, Elena, Eleni, Ellyn
NICKNAME: Ellie

**ELYSIA** *(Greek)* Blissful
VARIATION: Elsa
NICKNAME: Eli

**EMILY** *(English)* Industrious
VARIATIONS: Amelia, Emelia, Emme
NICKNAMES: Em, Emmie, Emmy

**EMMA** *(German)* Whole
VARIATION: Ema
NICKNAMES: Em, Emmie, Emmy

**ERICA** *(Scandinavian)* Leader
VARIATIONS: Ericka, Erika, Errika

**ERIN** *(Gaelic)* Ireland, peace
VARIATIONS: Errin, Eryn
NICKNAME: Eri

**ESPERANZA** *(Spanish)* Hope
NICKNAME: Espie

**ESTELLE** *(Latin)* Star

**ESTHER** *(Persian)* Myrtle leaf

**EUGENIA** *(Greek)* Well born
VARIATION: Eugenie

**EUNICE** *(Greek)* Happy

**EVE** *(Hebrew)* Breath of life
VARIATIONS: Evaline, Evelyn, Evelynne, Evonne
NICKNAMES: Ev, Eva, Evie

# F

**FADHILA** *(African)* Outstanding

**FAITH** *(English)* Loyalty, trust
VARIATIONS: Faithe, Faythe
NICKNAME: Fay

**FALLON** *(Irish)* Leader
VARIATION: Falon

**FARRAH** *(English)* Pleasant, beautiful
VARIATIONS: Farah, Farra

**FAY** *(French)* Fairy
VARIATION: Faye

**FELICIA** *(Latin)* Great happiness
VARIATIONS: Felice, Felicity

**FEODORA** *(Russian)* Gift from God

**FIONA** *(Celtic, Irish)* Fair
VARIATIONS: Fione, Fionna
NICKNAME: Fi

**FLORENCE** *(Latin)* Blossoming

**FONDA** *(French)* To melt
VARIATION: Fondea

**FRANCES** *(English, Latin)* From Franciscus, meaning "a free man"
VARIATIONS: Francine, Francis
NICKNAMES: Fannie, Frankie, Franny

**FRIEDA** *(German)* At peace
VARIATIONS: Freda, Fredda
NICKNAMES: Fredi, Fredie

# G

**GABRIELA** *(Hebrew)* Of God
VARIATIONS: Gabrella, Gabrielle
NICKNAMES: Gabbie, Gabby

**GAIL** *(Hebrew)* Father's joy
VARIATIONS: Gael, Gaile, Gale, Gayle

**GENEVIEVE** *(Celtic)* White
VARIATIONS: Genavieve, Geneva, Gina
NICKNAMES: Gennie, Genny, Jenny

**GEORGIA** *(Greek)* Female form of George, meaning "farm laborer"
VARIATIONS: Georgeanna, Georgette, Georgina
NICKNAME: Georgie

**GERALDINE** *(French)* Rules with a spear
VARIATIONS: Geraldeen, Geralynne, Jeraldene
NICKNAMES: Geri, Gerry, Jeri, Jerrie

**GIANNA** *(Italian)* Forgiving
VARIATION: Giana

**GILDA** *(English)* Covered in gold

**GILLIAN** *(Greek)* Youthful
VARIATION: Jillian
NICKNAME: Jill

**GIMBYA** *(African)* Princess

**GINA** *(Hebrew)* Garden
VARIATIONS: Geena, Gena, Ginia

**GINGER** *(English)* Peppy, lively

**GISELLE** *(English)* Oath, protector
VARIATIONS: Gisela, Gisele, Gisella, Gizela, Gizella
NICKNAME: Gigi

**GITA** *(Hindu)* Song
VARIATION: Geeta

**GLADYS** *(Welsh)* Princess

**GLENDA** *(Welsh)* Fair and mild
VARIATION: Gwendolen
NICKNAME: Glen

**GLORIA** *(Latin)* Praise, glory
VARIATIONS: Glori, Glorie, Glorria, Glory

**GRACE** *(Latin)* Attractive
VARIATIONS: Engracia, Gratia, Grazielle
NICKNAME: Gracie

**GREER** *(Latin)* Ever watching
VARIATION: Grier

**GRETA** *(Greek)* Pearlescent
VARIATION: Gretchen

**GUINEVERE** *(Welsh)* Fair
VARIATIONS: Gwendolyn, Gweneth, Gwenyth
NICKNAME: Gwen

**GWYNETH** *(Celtic)* Natural
VARIATIONS: Gweneth, Gwenyth
NICKNAMES: Gwen, Gwenna, Gwennie, Gwenny,
Gwynne, Winnie

# H

**HALLA** *(African)* Unexpected gift

**HANNAH** *(Hebrew)* Grace
VARIATION: Hanna

**HARMONY** *(Greek)* Agreement in feelings
VARIATIONS: Harmonia, Harmonie

**HAYLEY** *(English)* Meadow of hay
VARIATIONS: Hailey, Haley, Halie, Hallie, Hally,
Haylee

**HAZEL** *(English)* Powerful

**HEATHER** *(English)* Flowering, blooming

**HEIDI** *(German)* Noble, perky
VARIATIONS: Heide, Heidie

**HELEN** *(Greek)* Bright one
VARIATIONS: Helena, Helene, Helina

**HELKI** *(Native American)* Tender touch
VARIATIONS: Helkie, Helky

**HENRIETTA** *(German)* Leader of the home

**HERMIONE** *(Greek)* Speedy messenger
VARIATION: Hermina

**HIALEAH** *(Native American)* Beautiful pasture

**HILARY** *(Greek)* Cheerful
VARIATIONS: Hilarie, Hillary

**HISA** *(Japanese)* Everlasting

**HOLLY** *(English)* Holly tree or shrub
VARIATIONS: Hollie, Hollis

**HOPE** *(English)* To wish with optimism

# I

**IDA** *(English)* Youth
VARIATIONS: Aida, Idena, Ita

**IMENA** *(African)* Dream

**IMOGENE** *(Latin)* Image
VARIATIONS: Emogene, Imogen, Imogine
NICKNAMES: Immy, Jean

**INDIA** *(English)* The country of India
NICKNAME: Indy

**INGA** *(Scandinavian)* God of fertility
VARIATIONS: Inge, Ingrid

**IRENE** *(Greek)* Peace
VARIATIONS: Arina, Irena, Irina, Rene, Renee, Rina
NICKNAMES: Rennie, Renny

**ISABEL** *(Spanish)* Pledge of God
VARIATIONS: Isabella, Isabelle, Isobel
NICKNAMES: Belle, Issy, Izzy

# The Birds and the Bees

*Take a good look around. Our environment could be the muse for many lovely girls' names. Consider the following, inspired by nature:*

| | |
|---|---|
| Brooke | Honey |
| Chrysanthemum | Iris |
| Clover | Lark |
| Crystal | Lilac |
| Daffodil | Lily |
| Dahlia | Pansy |
| Daisy | Rose |
| Fawn | Skye |
| Fern | Star |
| Flora | Violet |
| Gazelle | Willow |
| Holly | Zinnia |

**ISADORA** *(Latin)* Gift of Isis
VARIATION: Isidora
NICKNAMES: Dora, Issy, Izzy

**ITALIA** *(Latin)* From Italy
NICKNAME: Talia

**ITO** *(Japanese)* Fiber

**IVANA** *(Slavic)* God is good
VARIATION: Ivanna

**IVORY** *(Latin)* Ivory
VARIATIONS: Ivoree, Ivorie

# J

**JACINTA** *(Spanish)* Hyacinth
VARIATIONS: Jacinda, Jacintha, Jacinthe, Jacinthia
NICKNAMES: Jacki, Jackie, Jacky, Jacqui

**JACQUELINE** *(French)* Female form of Jake,
meaning "follower"
VARIATIONS: Jackeline, Jacklyn,
Jaclyn, Jacquelyn
NICKNAMES: Jacki, Jackie

**JADE** *(Spanish)* Jade stone
VARIATIONS: Jada, Jaide, Jayde
NICKNAME: Jady

**JAMILA** *(African, Arabic)* Beautiful
VARIATION: Jamilla
NICKNAME: Jamie

**JANA** *(Slavic)* Form of Jane, meaning "believer in a gracious God"
VARIATION: Janna

**JANE** *(Old French, Hebrew)* Believer in a gracious God
VARIATIONS: Janet, Janice, Janine, Jayne, Jean, Joan, Joanne, Mary Jane, Sarah Jane
NICKNAMES: Janey, Jani

**JARDENA** *(Hebrew)* To flow downward
VARIATION: Jordana

**JASMINE** *(Persian)* Olive flower
VARIATIONS: Jasmin, Jasmina, Yasmin, Yasmina
NICKNAMES: Jazz, Jess

**JEMIMA** *(Hebrew)* Dove
NICKNAME: Jemma

**JENNA** *(Arabic)* Small bird
VARIATION: Jena

**JENNIFER** *(Welsh)* Smooth, soft
VARIATIONS: Gennifer, Ginnifer, Jenifer, Jenilee,
Jenilynn, Jennessa, Jennilyn
NICKNAMES: Jen, Jena, Jenn, Jenna, Jennie, Jenny

**JESSICA** *(Hebrew)* Wealthy
VARIATIONS: Jesica, Jesseca, Jessika
NICKNAMES: Jess, Jessie

**JEWEL** *(Latin, French)* Precious stone

**JILL** *(English)* Young
VARIATIONS: Gil, Gillian, Jil, Jillian, Jyl,
NICKNAME: Jillie

**JOAN** *(Hebrew)* God is gracious
NICKNAME: Joanie

**JOANNE** *(American)* Variant of Joan, meaning
"God is gracious"
VARIATIONS: Joanna, Jo Ann, Jo Anne, Johanna
NICKNAME: Jo

**JOCELYN** *(Latin)* Joyous, light-hearted

**JODY** *(Hebrew)* A woman from Judea
VARIATIONS: Jodene, Jodette, Jodi, Jodie
NICKNAME: Jo

**JOELLE** *(French)* God is Lord
VARIATIONS: Joell, Joellyn, Joely
NICKNAME: Jo

**JOHANNA** *(English)* God's grace
VARIATIONS: Joana, Joanna
NICKNAME: Jo

**JOLENE** *(American)* Contemporary version of Josephine, meaning "God will add"
VARIATIONS: Joleen, Jolione, Jolyn
NICKNAMES: Joli, Jolie

**JORDANA** *(Hebrew)* Down-flowing
VARIATION: Jordanna

**JOSEPHINE** *(Hebrew)* God will add
VARIATIONS: Josefa, Josefina, Josefine, Josepha, Josephene, Josephina, Josette
NICKNAMES: Jo, Jo-Jo, Josie

**JOY** *(Latin)* Merry
VARIATIONS: Joia, Joye

**JOYCE** *(Latin)* Joyous
VARIATION: Joice

**JUDITH** *(Hebrew)* Praise
VARIATION: Jodette
NICKNAMES: Judi, Judie, Judy

**JULIA** *(English)* Young
VARIATIONS: Juliana, Juliane, Julianna, Julianne, Juliette
NICKNAMES: Jules, Julie

**JUSTINE** *(Latin)* Female form of Justin, meaning "upright"
VARIATION: Justina
NICKNAME: Jussy

# K

**KAITLIN** *(Irish)* Pure
VARIATIONS: Caitlin, Caitlyn, Kaitlyn
NICKNAMES: Kat, Katie

**KALLI** *(Greek)* Lark
VARIATIONS: Calli, Callie, Kalia, Kallie

**KAMILI** *(African)* Perfection
VARIATIONS: Camila, Camile, Camili, Camille
NICKNAMES: Cami, Kami

**KAREN** *(Scandinavian)* From Katherine, meaning "pure"
VARIATIONS: Caren, Carin, Caryn, Kara, Karena, Karenna, Karin, Karine, Karon, Karyn, Keren

**KATHERINE** *(Greek)* Pure
VARIATIONS: Catherine, Katharin, Katharine, Katharyn, Kathleen, Kathlyn, Kathrine, Kathryn, Kathryne
NICKNAMES: Kate, Kathy, Katie, Kay, Kit, Kittie, Kitty

**KAYLA** *(English)* Pure
VARIATIONS: Cayla, Kaeli, Kaila, Kailee, Kailey, Kalee, Kali, Kayl
NICKNAME: Kaye

**KEESHA** *(African-American)* Dark-eyed
VARIATIONS: Keisha, Kiesha

**KENDRA** *(English)* Understanding

**KIA** *(African)* Season's beginning

**KIMBERLY** *(English)* King's meadow
VARIATIONS: Kimberlee, Kimberleigh, Kimberley
NICKNAMES: Kim, Kimmi, Kimmie

**KIRSTEN** *(Scandinavian, English)* Church
VARIATIONS: Kersten, Kiersten, Kirsta, Kirstin
NICKNAMES: Kersti, Kerstie, Kirsty

**KOKO** *(Japanese)* Stork
VARIATION: Coco

**KRISTIN** *(English)* Anointed
VARIATIONS: Krista, Kristan, Kristina, Kristine, Krysta
NICKNAME: Kris

**KYLIE** *(Scottish)* Female version of Kyle, meaning "narrow land"

**KYRA** *(Greek)* Enthroned
VARIATIONS: Cyra, Keira, Kira

# L

**LACEY** *(French)* Last name
VARIATIONS: Laci, Lacie, Lacy

**LANA** *(Latin)* Woolly
VARIATIONS: Lanette, Lanne
NICKNAMES: Laney, Lanny

**LARA** *(Roman)* Nymph daughter
VARIATION: Laura

**LARISSA** *(Greek)* Happy
VARIATIONS: Laresa, Laressa, Larisa

**LAURA** *(Latin)* Crowned with laurel

**LAUREL** *(Latin)* Bay tree
VARIATIONS: Laura, Laurette
NICKNAMES: Laurie, Lori

**LAUREN** *(English)* A form of Laura, meaning "crowned with laurel"

**LAURIE** *(English)* Familiar form of Laura
VARIATION: Lori

**LAYLA** *(African)* Born at night
VARIATION: Laila

**LEAH** *(Hebrew)* Weary
VARIATIONS: Lea, Lee, Leigh, Lia

**LEILA** *(Arabic)* Night beauty
VARIATION: Lila

**LENORE** *(Greek)* Light

**LEONA** *(Greek)* Female form of Leo, meaning "strength of character"
VARIATIONS: Leonia, Leonora

**LETIFA** *(Arabic, African)* Gentle
VARIATIONS: Latifa, Lateefah, Letipha
NICKNAMES: Tifa, Tifah

**LIANA** *(French)* To bind
VARIATIONS: Leana, Leanne, Lianna, Lianne

**LIESEL** *(German)* Variation of Elizabeth
VARIATIONS: Liesl, Liezl

**LINA** *(Arabic, Latin)* Palm tree
VARIATION: Lena

**LINDA** *(Latin)* Pretty

**LINDSAY** *(English)* Island of linden trees
VARIATIONS: Lindsey, Lyndsey
NICKNAME: Lynn

**LISA** *(English)* Short form of Elizabeth, meaning "oath of God"
VARIATIONS: Leesa, Leeza, Liza

**LISHA** *(African)* Mysterious

**LIZA** *(English)* Short form of Elizabeth and Eliza

43

**LOIS** *(Greek)* Good

**LOLA** *(English)* Sorrow
VARIATIONS: Loleta, Loletta, Lolita

**LORETTA** *(Latin)* Form of Laura, meaning "crowned with laurel"

**LORNA** *(Scottish)* Form of Laura, meaning "crowned with laurel"

**LORRAINE** *(French)* Section of France
NICKNAME: Rainey

**LOUISE** *(English)* Soldier
VARIATIONS: Louiza, Luisa
NICKNAMES: Lou, Lu, Lulu

**LUCIA** *(Latin)* To shine
VARIATIONS: Luciana, Lucienne, Lucinda, Lucine, Lucita, Luzine
NICKNAMES: Lu, Luci, Lucy

**LUCY** *(English)* Light
VARIATIONS: Lucetta, Lucie, Lucilla, Lucille, Lucinda

**LYDIA** *(Greek)* A woman from Lydia
VARIATIONS: Lidia, Lydda
NICKNAME: Lydie

**LYNN** *(English)* Brook
VARIATIONS: Lin, Linne, Linnette, Lyn, Lynne

# M

**MABEL** *(Latin)* Loveable
VARIATION: Maybelle

**MADELINE** *(Greek)* Woman from Magdala
VARIATION: Madeleine
NICKNAMES: Maddie, Maddy

**MAEVE** *(Irish)* Joy

**MALICA** *(African)* Queen
NICKNAME: Mallie

**MALLORY** *(French)* Unfortunate
VARIATIONS: Mallorey, Mallorie, Malorie, Malory

**MANICA** *(African)* From the Nica

**MARA** *(Hebrew)* Bitter
VARIATIONS: Marah,
Mariah, Marra

**MARGARET** *(English)* Pearl
VARIATIONS: Margareta, Margaretta, Margarette, Margarita, Margarite, Margeret, Margerey, Margot, Marguerite, Meagan, Meaghan, Megan, Meghan, Meghann
NICKNAMES: Greta, Maggie, Mags, Marge, Meg, Meggie, Meggy, Peg, Peggy

**MARGO** *(French)* Form of Margaret, meaning "pearl"
VARIATIONS: Margaux, Margot

**MARIAH** *(Hebrew)* God is my teacher

**MARIAN** *(French)* Form of Mary
VARIATION: Marion

**MARIBEL** *(Latin)* Beautiful Mary
VARIATION: Mary Belle

**MARIEL** *(Danish)* Star of the sea

**MARILYN** *(English)* From Mary, meaning "descendants of Mary"
VARIATIONS: Maralyn, Marilee, Marilynn, Marylin
NICKNAMES: Mar, Merry

**MARINA** *(Latin)* Of the sea
VARIATIONS: Maren, Maris, Marisa, Marissa, Marne, Marni
NICKNAME: Rina

**MARINI** *(Swahili)* Pretty

**MARISOL** *(Latin)* Sunny sea

**MARISSA** *(Latin)* Sea born
VARIATIONS: Maris, Marisa

**MARJORIE** *(English)* Form of Margaret, meaning "pearl"

**MARQUITA** *(French)* Canopy
VARIATION: Marquite

**MARSHA** *(Latin)* Dedicated to Mars
VARIATIONS: Marcella, Marcia, Marcy

**MARTHA** *(Aramaic)* Lady
VARIATIONS: Em, Marly, Marta, Martina

**MARY** *(English)* From the Hebrew name, Miriam, meaning "child of our wishes"
VARIATIONS: Mari, Maria, Marie, Mariel, Mariette, Marion, Marita, Maura, Mira

**MAURA** *(Celtic)* Variant of Mary, meaning "dark"

**MAUREEN** *(Irish)* Variant of Mary, meaning "dark"

# Fifteen Minutes of Fame

*When a celebrity has an unusual name, it often sparks the interest of parents-to-be. In the '70s, girls' names like "Farrah" and "Tatum" were trendy. The '80s brought us uncommon female monikers like "Demi," "Margot," and "Glenn." And in the '90s, we heard the new names "Calista" and "Latifah." Current red hot celebrity names to look at include:*

| | |
|---|---|
| Ashlee | Fantasia |
| Avril | Gwenyth |
| Beyoncé | Paris |
| Ciara | Reese |
| Drew | Scarlet |

**MAYA** *(Greek)* Great mother

**MEAGAN** *(Welsh)* Variant of Margaret, meaning "pearl"
VARIATION: Megan

**MELANIE** *(Greek)* Dark complexion
VARIATIONS: Malina, Melana, Melina, Mellanie, Milena
NICKNAMES: Mel, Mellie

**MELINDA** *(Latin)* Sweet

**MELISSA** *(Greek)* Bee, implying sweetness
VARIATIONS: Malissa, Melessa, Melisa, Misha
NICKNAME: Missy

**MELODY** *(Greek)* Tune
VARIATION: Melina
NICKNAME: Mel

**MEREDITH** *(Welsh)* Great leader
VARIATIONS: Meri, Meridith
NICKNAMES: Merrie, Merry

**MERYL** *(English)* Bright as the sea
VARIATIONS: Merill, Merrell, Merrill, Meryle

**MIA** *(Italian)* Mine

**MICHAELA** *(Hebrew)* Female form of Michael, which means "Who is like God?"
VARIATIONS: Makaela, Micaela, Michael, Michaella, Michele, Michelina, Michelle, Mykayla
NICKNAMES: Mickie, Micky, Mike

**MICHELLE** *(French, Hebrew)* Who resembles god
VARIATION: Michele

**MILDRED** *(English)* Mild
NICKNAME: Millie

**MIRANDA** *(Latin)* Amazing
VARIATIONS: Marenda, Mira, Myranda
NICKNAMES: Randee, Randey, Randi, Randie, Randy

**MIRIAM** *(Hebrew)* She who knows her own way

**MOLLY** *(English)* From Margaret, meaning "pearl"
VARIATION: Mollie

**MONA** *(Greek)* Alone;
*(Arabic)* Wish
VARIATIONS: Monica, Monique

**MYRA** *(Latin)* Fragrant
VARIATIONS: Moira, Myrah

# N

**NABILA** *(African)* Noble

**NADIA** *(Russian)* Hope
VARIATIONS: Nada, Nadeen,
Nadene, Nadina, Nadine, Nadja
NICKNAMES: Nadie, Nady

**NAIMA** *(African)* Graceful

**NANCY** *(Hebrew)* Grace
VARIATIONS: Nancee, Nancey, Nancie
NICKNAMES: Nan, Nance, Nannie

**NAOMI** *(Hebrew)* Delightful
VARIATIONS: Naoma, Noemi
NICKNAME: Nomi

**NATALIE** *(Latin)* Birthday
VARIATIONS: Natalee, Natalia, Natasha, Natelie
NICKNAME: Nat

**NATASHA** *(Greek)* Rebirth
VARIATIONS: Nastassia, Nastassja

**NELL** *(English)* Light
VARIATION: Nella
NICKNAMES: Nelli, Nellie, Nelly

**NICHELLE** *(African-American)* Victorious maiden

**NICOLE** *(English, Greek)* People of victory
VARIATIONS: Nichelle, Nichola, Nichole, Nicolette, Nicolle
NICKNAMES: Nicki, Nickie, Nicky, Nikki

**NINA** *(Spanish)* Little girl
VARIATIONS: Neena, Ninetta, Ninette, Ninnette, Nona, Nynette

**NOELANI** *(Hawaiian)* Beautiful girl from heaven

**NOELLE** *(French)* Christmas
VARIATIONS: Noel, Noele, Noell, Noella

**NOLA** *(English)* White shoulder
VARIATIONS: Nolah, Nolana

**NORA** *(Greek)* Light
VARIATIONS: Norah, Noreen

# O

**OCTAVIA** *(Latin)* Eight
VARIATIONS: Octavie, Ottavia
NICKNAMES: Tavi, Tavia

**ODELIA** *(Greek)* Song
VARIATIONS: Odele, Odetta
NICKNAME: Detta

**OLGA** *(Norse, Scandinavian)* Blessed
VARIATION: Helga

**OLIVIA** *(Latin)* Olive tree
VARIATIONS: Oliva, Olive
NICKNAMES: Liv, Ollie

**OLYMPIA** *(Greek)* Heavenly
VARIATION: Olympias

**ONAWA** *(Native American)* Wide-awake girl

**OPAL** *(Sanskrit)* Precious stone
VARIATIONS: Opalina, Opaline

**OPHELIA** *(Greek)* Help

**OPRAH** *(Hebrew)* Fawn, young and delicate

**ORIANA** *(Latin)* Rising sun
VARIATION: Oriane

**ORLENE** *(French)* Golden

**ORLEY** *(Hebrew)* My light
VARIATIONS: Orlee, Orli

# P

**PAIGE** *(Greek, Italian)* Child, assistant
VARIATION: Page

**PAKA** *(African)* Cat

**PALOMA** *(Latin)* Dove
VARIATION: Palometa

**PAMELA** *(Greek)* Honey
VARIATIONS: Pamala, Pamalia, Pamelia, Pamella, Pamilia
NICKNAMES: Pam, Pammi, Pammie, Pammy

# Initial Reaction

Fiona Ann Thomas is a pretty enough name, but she surely won't appreciate it when her classmates figure out that her initials spell "FAT." Parents often forget to think about the set of initials they're creating for their new family member. When you come up with a name for your baby, think about how the initials will one day look on an engraved keychain. You might then opt for your second choice.

**PARIS** *(English)* The city of Paris
VARIATIONS: Parisa, Parris

**PATIENCE** *(Latin)* Endurance
VARIATION: Patia

**PATRICIA** *(English)* Noble
VARIATIONS: Patrice, Patricka, Patrizia
NICKNAMES: Pat, Patti, Patsy, Patty, Tricia, Trish,
Trisha

**PAULA** *(Latin)* Small
VARIATIONS: Paola, Pauletta, Paulette, Paulina,
Pauline, Pavlina
NICKNAME: Polly

**PEARL** *(Latin)* Jewel from the sea

**PENELOPE** *(Greek)* Weaver
VARIATIONS: Penelopa, Pennelope
NICKNAMES: Nell, Nellie, Penni, Penny

**PERDITA** *(Latin)* Lost
NICKNAMES: Perdie, Perdy

**PERLA** *(Italian, Spanish)* Pearl
VARIATIONS: Pearl, Pearla, Pearlette, Pearline, Perle

**PETRA** *(Greek)* Female form of Peter, meaning "rock"
VARIATIONS: Peta, Petrina, Petronia
NICKNAMES: Pet, Petie, Petty

**PHILIPPA** *(Greek)* Horse-lover
VARIATIONS: Felipa, Philippine, Phillippa
NICKNAMES: Philli, Philly, Pip, Pippa, Pippy

**PHOEBE** *(Greek)* Radiant

**PHYLLIS** *(Greek)* Green branch
NICKNAME: Phil

**PIA** *(Latin)* Faithful

**PILAR** *(Latin)* Pillar

**PIPER** *(American)* One who plays pipes

**PORTIA** *(Latin)* Name of ancient Roman clan
VARIATIONS: Porscha, Porschia, Porsha

**PRISCILLA** *(English)* Old-fashioned
VARIATIONS: Precilla, Pricilla, Priscila
NICKNAMES: Cilla, Pris, Prissie, Prissy

**PRUDENCE** *(English)* Caution and wisdom

# Q

**QUEENIE** *(English)* Woman ruler
VARIATION: Queena

**QUINN** *(Irish)* Smart, advisor

**QUINTA** *(Latin)* Fifth
VARIATIONS: Quintilla, Quintina

**QUINTESSA** *(Latin)* Essence
NICKNAME: Tess

# R

**RACHEL** *(Hebrew)* Gentle lamb
VARIATIONS: Rachael, Racheal, Rachele, Rachelle,
Raquel, Raquela, Raquelle
NICKNAMES: Rach, Ray, Raye

**RAFAELA** *(Spanish)* God heals
VARIATIONS: Rafeala, Rafella, Rephaela
NICKNAME: Raffi

**RAFIYA** *(African)* Dignified

**RAINE** *(Latin)* Authority
VARIATIONS: Raina, Rayna, Reyna
NICKNAME: Rainey

**RAISA** *(African)* Exalted
VARIATION: Raysa

**RAMONA** *(Spanish)* Protector
VARIATION: Romona
NICKNAME: Mona

**RAYNA** *(Yiddish)* Pure
VARIATIONS: Raina, Rania, Reyna
NICKNAME: Ray

**REBECCA** *(Hebrew)* Faithful wife
VARIATIONS: Rebbecca, Rebeca, Rebeccah, Rebecka,
Rebeckah, Rebeka, Rebekah, Rebekka
NICKNAMES: Becca, Becky

**REGINA** *(Latin)* Queen
VARIATIONS: Regine, Reina
NICKNAMES: Reggi, Reggie

**RHIANNON** *(Welsh)* Goddess
VARIATIONS: Rheanna, Rhiana, Rianna, Rianne,
Riannon

**RHODA** *(Greek)* Rose
VARIATIONS: Rhona, Rhonda, Roda
NICKNAME: Rhody

**RINAKO** *(Japanese)* Child of Rina

**RISA** *(Latin)* Laughter
VARIATIONS: Reesa, Resa

**RITA** *(Indian)* Brave
VARIATION: Rheta

**ROBERTA** *(English)* Fame
VARIATIONS: Robin, Robyn
NICKNAMES: Bobbi, Bobbie, Robbi, Robbie, Robby

**ROCHELLE** *(French)* Little rock
VARIATIONS: Rochele, Rochell, Rochella

**ROHANA** *(Hindu)* Sandalwood

**ROLANDA** *(German)* Famous land
VARIATIONS: Rolaine, Rolande, Rolene

**ROMY** *(Latin)* Short form of Rosemary, meaning "dew of the sea"
VARIATION: Roma

**ROSALIND** *(Latin)* Pretty rose
VARIATIONS: Rosaleen, Rosalin, Rosalinda, Rosaline, Rosalyn, Rosalynd, Rosamond, Roseleen, Roselyn, Rossalyn
NICKNAMES: Rose, Roz

**ROSE** *(Latin)* Rose flower

**ROSEANNE** *(English)* Combination of Rose and Anne
VARIATION: Rosanne

**ROSEMARY** *(Latin)* Dew of the sea
VARIATIONS: Rosemarie
NICKNAMES: Ro, Rose

**ROWAN** *(English)* Red berry tree
VARIATION: Rowen

**ROWENA** *(Celtic)* Fair
NICKNAME: Ro

**ROXANNE** *(Persian)* Dawn
VARIATIONS: Rosana, Roxane, Roxanna
NICKNAMES: Roxie, Roxy

**RUBY** *(English)* Jewel
VARIATIONS: Rubey, Rubie

# T. J. is Okay

If you like "Max," but not "Maximilian," or "Pat," but not "Patricia," fear not. The new rule is—anything goes!

Shortened versions of longer, more traditional names are becoming mainstream. You might choose "Ali" over Alison, "Kate" over Katherine, or "Abby" over "Abigail" for your daughter. Likewise, "Mac" can replace "Macmillan" for your boy, "Jack" is no longer just short for "Jackson," and "Chip" can work as well as "Charles." Some other popular nicknames that are making their way onto birth certificates include Billie, Joe, Camie, and Tess.

**RUMER** *(English)* Gypsy name

**RUTH** *(Hebrew)* Friend
VARIATIONS: Ruthe, Ruthelle
NICKNAMES: Ruthi, Ruthie, Ruthy

# S

**SAADA** *(African)* Helper
VARIATION: Sada
NICKNAMES: Sadie, Sady

**SABRA** *(African)* Patience

**SABRINA** *(Arabic, Hebrew)* Thorny cactus
VARIATIONS: Sabine, Sabra, Zabrina

**SADIE** *(English)* Seed
VARIATION: Sady

**SAGE** *(English)* Wise one

**SAHARA** *(Arabic)* Desert

**SAKARA** *(Native American)* Sweet

**SAKURA** *(Japanese)* Cherry blossom

**SALENA** *(Greek)* Goddess of the moon
VARIATIONS: Celena, Celina, Celine, Celyna, Salina,
Sela, Selene, Selina

**SALLY** *(Hebrew)* Princess
VARIATIONS: Saliee, Sallie
NICKNAME: Sal

**SALMA** *(Arabic)* Safe

**SAMANTHA** *(Aramaic)* One who listens
NICKNAMES: Sam, Sami, Samie, Sammy

**SAMARA** *(Latin)* Elm seed

**SAMIRA** *(Arabic)* Entertaining

**SANDRA** *(Greek)* Helper of humanity
VARIATION: Sondra
NICKNAMES: Sandy, Sondi

**SARA** *(Hebrew)* Princess
VARIATION: Sarah

**SASCHA** *(Russian)* Form of Alexandra, meaning "one who defends"
VARIATION: Sasha

**SAVANNAH** *(Spanish)* Treeless
VARIATIONS: Savanah, Savanna

**SCARLET** *(English)* Red
VARIATIONS: Scarlett, Scarlette

**SELA** *(Hebrew)* Rock

**SELMA** *(Celtic)* Fair
VARIATION: Zelma

**SERAPHINA** *(Hebrew)* To burn
VARIATIONS: Serafina, Seraphine

**SERENA** *(Latin)* Clear, serene
VARIATIONS: Sarena, Sarina, Serenah, Serina

**SHANI** *(Swahili)* Marvelous

**SHANNON** *(Irish)* Ancient
VARIATION: Shanon

**SHARON** *(Hebrew)* Flat area
VARIATIONS: Shaaron, Sharyn

**SHEILA** *(Irish)* Blind

**SHELBY** *(English)* Estate
VARIATIONS: Shelbee, Shelbey
NICKNAME: Shel

**SHERRY** *(English)* Variant of Chérie, meaning "dear"

**SHIFRA** *(Hebrew)* Beautiful
VARIATION: Schifra

**SHIRLEY** *(English)* Meadow
VARIATIONS: Sherlee, Sherline, Sheryl, Shirleen, Shirline
NICKNAME: Shirl

**SHUKUMA** *(African)* Be grateful

**SIBYL** *(Greek)* Oracle, prophetess
VARIATIONS: Sibbell, Sibel, Sibelle, Sibyll, Sybel, Sybil, Sybill, Sybyl

**SIENNA** *(Latin)* Italian city, brownish-red

**SIMONE** *(French)* God listens
VARIATIONS: Simona, Simonette, Symone

**SONIA** *(Russian)* Variant of Sophia, meaning "wisdom"
VARIATION: Sonja

**SOPHIA** *(Greek)* Wisdom
VARIATIONS: Sofi, Sofia, Sophey, Sophie, Sophy, Zofia

**STELLA** *(Latin)* Star

**STEPHANIE** *(English)* Crown
VARIATIONS: Stefanie, Stephannie, Stephenie
NICKNAMES: Steffi, Stevi, Stevie

**SUKI** *(Japanese)* Beloved

**SUSAN** *(Hebrew)* Lily
VARIATIONS: Susann, Susanna, Susannah, Susanne, Susette, Suzan, Suzane, Suzanna, Suzannah, Suzanne, Suzette
NICKNAMES: Sue, Susi, Susie, Susy, Suzi, Suzie

**SYLVIA** *(Latin)* Woods, forest

# T

**TABITHA** *(English)* Graceful as a gazelle
VARIATIONS: Tabatha, Tabbitha, Tabetha
NICKNAME: Tabby

**TALIA** *(Hebrew)* Dew
VARIATION: Talya
NICKNAMES: Talie, Talley, Tallie, Tally

**TALLULAH** *(Native American)* Running water
VARIATIONS: Tallula, Talula, Talulah, Talulla

**TAMARA** *(Hebrew)* Palm tree

**TANDICE** *(African-American)* Team
NICKNAME: Tandy

**TANYA** *(Russian)* Fairy queen
VARIATION: Tania

**TARA** *(Irish)* Hill
VARIATIONS: Tarah, Tarra, Tarrah, Tarryn, Taryn

**TATUM** *(English)* Female form of Tate, meaning "cheerful"
NICKNAMES: Tata, Tate

**TEMPERANCE** *(Latin)* Moderation

**TEMPEST** *(French)* Storm

**TESS** *(English)* Variant of Teresa
VARIATION: Tessa

**THELMA** *(Greek)* Willful

**THEODORA** *(Greek)* God-given

**THERESA** *(Greek)* To harvest
VARIATIONS: Terasa, Teresa, Teresia, Teressa, Terise,
Therese
NICKNAMES: Teri, Terie, Terri, Terrie, Terry

**TIA** *(Greek)* Princess
VARIATION: Téa

**TIFFANY** *(Greek)* Divine manifestation
VARIATIONS: Tifani, Tiffaney, Tiffani, Tiffanie,
Tiffiney, Tiffini, Tiffney, Tyfanny
NICKNAMES: Tiff, Tiffy

**TISHA** *(African)* Strong willed

**TRICIA** *(English)* Variant of Patricia, meaning
"noble"
VARIATION: Trisha
NICKNAME: Trish

**TRISTA** *(English)* Melancholy

**TYRA** *(English)* Assertive

**TYRONICA** *(African-American)*
Goddess of Battle

# U

**ULTIMA** *(Latin)* Winner

**UMA** *(Hebrew)* Nation; *(Sanskrit)* Light and peace

**UNA** *(Irish)* Lamb
VARIATION: Oona

**URSULA** *(Latin)* Little female bear
VARIATIONS: Ursala, Ursella, Ursuline

# V

**VALERIE** *(Latin)* Strong, healthy
VARIATIONS: Valaree, Valarey, Valari, Valeria,
Vallarie, Valleree, Vallerie
NICKNAME: Val

**VANESSA** *(Greek)* Butterflies
VARIATIONS: Vanesa, Vannessa, Venesa, Venessa
NICKNAME: Nessa

**VANNA** *(Cambodian)* Golden

**VENUS** *(Latin)* Love
VARIATIONS: Venise, Vennice
NICKNAMES: Vin, Vinnie, Vinny

**VERA** *(Russian)* Faith
VARIATIONS: Veira, Viera

**VERONICA** *(Latin)* True image
VARIATIONS: Veronicka, Veronika, Veronique
NICKNAMES: Roni, Ronni, Ronnie, Vonnie

**VESTA** *(Roman)* Goddess of the home

**VICTORIA** *(Latin)* Victorious
VARIATIONS: Vitoria, Vittoria
NICKNAMES: Vici, Vick, Vicki, Vickie, Vicky

**VIOLA** *(Italian)* A four-stringed instrument, a flower
VARIATIONS: Violet, Violetta
NICKNAME: Vi

**VIRGINIA** *(Latin)* Virgin
VARIATIONS: Vergenia, Virginie
NICKNAMES: Ginger, Ginnie, Ginny, Virgie

**VITA** *(Latin)* Life
VARIATION: Vida

**VIVIAN** *(Latin)* Full of life
VARIATIONS: Viveca, Viviane,
Vivianna, Vivianne
NICKNAME: Viv

**WAKANDA** *(Sioux)* Magical power within

**WALLIS** *(English)* Choice
VARIATIONS: Walliss, Wallys
NICKNAMES: Wallie, Wally

**WANDA** *(Old Norse)* Slender stick
VARIATIONS: Vanda, Wenda, Wendeline

**WENDY** *(English)* Modern name invented by play-
wright James Barrie in *Peter Pan*
VARIATION: Wanda
NICKNAME: Wen

**WILHELMINA** *(German)* Female form of William, meaning "protector"
VARIATIONS: Willamina, Williamina
NICKNAMES: Wil, Willie

**WINIFRED** *(Welsh)* Peaceful woman
NICKNAME: Winnie

**WINNA** *(African)* Friend
NICKNAME: Winnie

**WINONA** *(Native American)* First-born daughter
VARIATIONS: Wenona, Wenonah, Winona, Winonah, Wynnona, Wynonah
NICKNAME: Winnie

# X

**XENA** *(Greek)* Guest from afar

**XENIA** *(Greek)* Hospitable
VARIATION: Xena

**XIOMARA** *(Spanish)* Agreeable

**XYLOPHILA** *(Greek)* Lover of forests
VARIATION: Xylona

# Y

**YANA** *(Slavic)* Lovely
VARIATIONS: Yanah, Yanni, Yanny

**YASMINE** *(Arabic)* Flower
VARIATIONS: Jasmin, Jasmine, Yasmin, Yasmina

**YELENA** *(Russian)* Light
VARIATION: Yalena

**YOKO** *(Japanese)* Child of the ocean

**YOLANDA** *(Latin)* Modest
VARIATIONS: Yolande, Yolette
NICKNAME: Yoli

**YUKI** *(Japanese)* Lucky
VARIATIONS: Yukie, Yukiko

**YVETTE** *(French)* Arrow's bow
VARIATION: Yvetta
NICKNAME: Yve

**YVONNE** *(French)* Yew wood
VARIATION: Yvone
NICKNAME: Yve

# Z

**ZADA** *(Arabic)* Fortunate

**ZALIKA** *(African)* Well born

**ZARA** *(Hebrew)* Dawn
VARIATIONS: Zarah, Zaria

**ZAWADI** *(African)* Gift

**ZENA** *(English)* Hospitable
VARIATIONS: Zenia, Zina

**ZEPHIRA** *(Hebrew)* Morning

**ZITA** *(Spanish)* Rose

**ZOE** *(Greek)* From Eve, meaning "breath of life"
VARIATIONS: Zoey, Zoie

**ZORA** *(Slavic)* Dawn
VARIATIONS: Zorah, Zorra, Zorrah

# Boys' Names

*A fairly bright boy is far more
intelligent and far better company
than the average adult.*

J. B. S. HALDANE

 "I want to become a boy, no matter how hard it is!" says a determined Pinocchio in the classic story by Carlo Collodi.

That famous wooden puppet must have known how wonderful little boys are. They  can be tough, funny, and sweet all at the same time. Give your baby boy a name that will express all aspects of his personality. Here are some great choices.

# A

**AARON** *(Hebrew)* Sing, shine, exalted one
VARIATIONS: Aron, Arran, Arron
NICKNAMES: Ari, Arnie, Ron, Ronnie, Ronny

**ABDUL** *(Arabic)* Servant of
VARIATIONS: Abdal, Abdel, Abul

**ABRAHAM** *(Hebrew)* Father of many
VARIATIONS: Abram, Avram
NICKNAMES: Ab, Abe, Ham

**ADAM** *(Hebrew)* Of the red earth
VARIATIONS: Adams, Adamson, Addam, Addison
NICKNAMES: Addie, Addy, Eddie

**ADOLPH** *(Old German)* Noble wolf
VARIATIONS: Adolf, Adolpho, Adolphus

**AHMED** *(Swahili)* Praiseworthy
VARIATIONS: Ahmad, Amad, Amed

**AJANI** *(African)* The victor

**ALAN** *(Celtic)* Handsome
VARIATIONS: Alain, Alano, Aleyn, Allan, Allen
NICKNAME: Al

**ALBERT** *(German)* Noble
VARIATIONS: Alberto, Albrecht
NICKNAMES: Al, Albie, Bert

**ALEXANDER** *(Greek)* Protector
VARIATIONS: Alastair, Alejandro, Aleksei, Alessander,
Alessandro, Alexandre, Alexius, Ali, Alistair,
Allesandro, Allistair
NICKNAMES: Al, Alec, Alek, Alex, Sandy

**ALFRED** *(Old English)* Counselor
VARIATIONS: Alfrey, Alfredo, Avery, Fred
NICKNAMES: Al, Alf, Alfie, Freddie, Fredo

**ALPHONSE** *(German)* Noble and eager
VARIATIONS: Alonzo, Alfonso, Alphonso
NICKNAMES: Al, Alfie, Alfons, Fons

**ALVIN** *(German)* Friend
VARIATIONS: Alwin, Elwin
NICKNAMES: Al, Alvie, Alvy

**ANDREW** *(English)* Brave
VARIATIONS: Anders, Andersen, Anderson, Andre,
Andreas, Andrei, Andros
NICKNAME: Andy

**ANGEL** *(Greek)* Messenger
VARIATIONS: Angelo, Angelos

**ANTHONY** *(Latin)* Valuable
VARIATIONS: Antoine, Anton, Antone, Antoni,
Antonio, Antony
NICKNAME: Tony

**ARNOLD** *(Old German)* Eagle ruler
VARIATIONS: Arnaldo, Arnaud, Arnauld, Arnault
NICKNAMES: Arn, Arne, Arney, Arnie

**ARTHUR** *(Gaelic)* Rock
VARIATIONS: Arturo, Artus
NICKNAMES: Art, Artie, Arty

**ASHER** *(Hebrew)* Happy
VARIATIONS: Ashford, Ashley
NICKNAME: Ash

**ASHTON** *(Old English)* Ash
tree town
VARIATIONS: Ashford, Aston
NICKNAME: Ash

**ATTICUS** *(Greek)* A region in Ancient Greece, associated with purity and elegance
VARIATIONS: Attica, Attila

**AUSTIN** *(English)* Majestic
VARIATION: Austen

**AVI** *(Hebrew)* My father

**AXEL** *(German)* Oak
VARIATION: Aksel

# B

**BALDWIN** *(German)* Bold
VARIATIONS: Boden, Bowden

**BARD** *(Gaelic)* Singing poet
VARIATIONS: Baird, Barton

**BARKER** *(English)* Birch
VARIATION: Barksdale
NICKNAME: Birk

**BARNABAS** *(Hebrew)* Comforter
VARIATION: Barnaby, Barnebas
NICKNAME: Barney

**BARRY** *(Celtic)* Good marksman
VARIATIONS: Barnard, Barrett, Barrington, Barris,
Barrymore

**BASIL** *(Greek)* Royal
VARIATION: Basile
NICKNAME: Baz

**BEAU** *(French)* Handsome
VARIATION: Bo

**BENEDICT** *(Latin)* To bless
VARIATIONS: Benedetto, Benedicto, Benett, Benito,
Beniton, Bennet, Bennett
NICKNAMES: Ben, Benny

**BENJAMIN** *(Hebrew)* Son of my right hand
VARIATIONS: Benjaman, Benjamon
NICKNAMES: Ben, Benjy, Benny

**BENSON** *(English)* Son of Ben
VARIATIONS: Bensen, Benssen, Bensson, Bentley,
Bently
NICKNAMES: Ben, Beny

BERNARD *(German)* Bold, brave
VARIATIONS: Barnard, Barnet, Barnett, Barney,
Barnhard, Barny, Barret, Barrett, Bernardino,
Bernardo, Bernhard, Bernhardt, Burnard
NICKNAMES: Barnie, Barny, Barr, Bern, Bernie,
Berny

BERT *(Old English)* Illustrious
VARIATION: Bertram
NICKNAMES: Bertie, Burt

BORIS *(Russian, Slavic)* Fighter
VARIATIONS: Boriss, Borris, Borys

BOYD *(Celtic)* Yellow-haired
VARIATIONS: Boid, Bowen
NICKNAME: Bowie

BRADLEY *(English)* Wide meadow
VARIATIONS: Braden, Bradford, Bradlee, Bradleigh,
Bradly, Brady
NICKNAMES: Brad, Lee

BRANDON *(English)* Fire
VARIATIONS: Brandan, Branden, Brandin, Brandt,
Brandyn, Brannt
NICKNAMES: Bran, Brand

**BRAXTON** *(English)* Brock's town
VARIATION: Brock

**BRENDAN** *(Irish)* Little raven
VARIATIONS: Breandan, Brenden, Brendin, Brendon, Brennan, Brennon, Brent
NICKNAMES: Bran, Bren

**BRIAN** *(Celtic, Greek)* Strong
VARIATIONS: Briant, Briar, Brien, Brion, Bryan, Bryant, Bryon

**BRIGHAM** *(English)* Covered bridge
VARIATIONS: Brighton, Brigman

**BRODERICK** *(Scottish)* Brother
VARIATIONS: Broderic, Brodric, Brodrick
NICKNAME: Brod

**BRONSON** *(English)* Dark man's son
VARIATIONS: Bronnson, Bronse, Bronsin, Bronsson
NICKNAME: Bron

**BRUCE** *(English)* Thick brush
VARIATIONS: Bruis, Bryson
NICKNAMES: Brice, Bryce, Brucie

**BUD** *(English)* Messenger
VARIATIONS: Budd, Buddy

**BYRD** *(English)* Young bird
VARIATIONS: Bird, Burdette

# C

**CALEB** *(Hebrew)* Brave
VARIATION: Kaleb
NICKNAMES: Cal, Cale

**CALVIN** *(French)* Bold
VARIATIONS: Calvino, Kalvin
NICKNAME: Cal

**CAMDEN** *(Scottish)* Winding valley
VARIATION: Camdon
NICKNAME: Cam

**CARL** *(English)* Man
VARIATIONS: Carden, Carter, Karl

**CARLOS** *(Spanish)* Manly
VARIATIONS: Carlino, Carlo, Carolo

**CARSON** *(Scottish, Old English)* Son of the
marsh-dwellers
NICKNAME: Carr

**CARTER** *(Old English)* One who transports goods
VARIATIONS: Cartier, Cartrell

**CESAR** *(Spanish)* Leader
VARIATIONS: Cesare, Cesaro

**CHAD** *(English)* Protector
VARIATIONS: Chadd, Chadwick

**CHANCE** *(English)* Good fortune
VARIATIONS: Chancello, Chandler, Chaney

**CHARLES** *(English)* Man
VARIATIONS: Carleton, Carlson, Carlton, Charlton
NICKNAMES: Char, Charley, Charlie, Chas, Chaz,
Chick, Chip, Chuck

**CHASE** *(English)* Hunter
VARIATIONS: Chace, Chasin, Chason

**CHEN** *(Chinese)* Great

**CHESTER** *(Old English, Latin)* Camp of soldiers
VARIATIONS: Chess, Cheston
NICKNAME: Chet

**CHRISTIAN** *(Greek)* Follower of Christ
VARIATIONS: Christan, Christer, Christie, Christo, Christos, Cristos
NICKNAMES: Chris, Kit, Kris

**CHRISTOPHER** *(English)* One who knows Christ
VARIATIONS: Christobal, Christof, Christofer, Christoff, Christoffer, Christoforus, Christoph, Christophe, Christophoros, Christos, Cristoforo, Kristofer, Kristofor, Kristopher
NICKNAMES: Chris, Cris, Kip, Kris

**CLARK** *(English)* Scholar
VARIATIONS: Clarke, Clerc, Clerk

**CLAUDIUS** *(Latin)* Limping
VARIATIONS: Claudian, Claudio
NICKNAMES: Claud, Claude, Claus

**CLAY** *(English)* Maker of clay
VARIATIONS: Clayton, Klay

**CLEMENT** *(Scottish)* Gentle
NICKNAME: Clem

**CLIFFORD** *(English)* A river-crossing
VARIATIONS: Clifton, Clyfford
NICKNAMES: Clif, Cliff, Clyff

**CLINTON** *(English)* Town on top of a hill
NICKNAME: Clint

# Role Models

*Who are your heroes? Lincoln?
Roosevelt? These and other names
borrowed from some of history's
leaders can be a unique inspiration
for your little boy's first name. Here
are some to get the wheels turning:*

| | |
|---|---|
| Caesar | Luther |
| Carter | Lyndon |
| Dwight | Mandela |
| Ford | Reagan |
| Franklin | Truman |
| Grant | Ulysses |
| Jefferson | Washington |
| Kennedy | Woodrow |

**CLIVE** *(English)* Steep
VARIATIONS: Cleavon, Cleve, Cleveland, Clyde
NICKNAMES: Clif, Cliff

**CLYDE** *(Welsh)* Adventurer
VARIATION: Clydell

**COLBY** *(Norse)* Dark country
VARIATION: Colbert

**COLE** *(Middle English, Old French)* Swarthy, coal-black, charcoal.
VARIATIONS: Coley, Colson

**COLIN** *(English)* Triumphant
VARIATIONS: Colan, Collin, Colyn, Colwyn
NICKNAME: Cole

**CONAN** *(Irish)* High
VARIATIONS: Conant, Kynan
NICKAME: Connie

**COOPER** *(Latin)* Barrel repairer
NICKNAME: Coop

COSMO *(Greek)* In harmony
VARIATIONS: Cosimo, Cosmé, Kosmo

CRAIG *(Welsh)* Of the rocks
VARIATION: Kraig

CRANE *(English)* To stretch
VARIATIONS: Crandall, Crandell

CURTIS *(Latin)* Courtyard
VARIATIONS: Courtland, Courtlandt, Courtney
NICKNAMES: Curt, Kurt

# D

DALAI *(Indian)* Peaceful
VARIATION: Dalee

DALE *(English)* Valley
VARIATION: Dayle

DAMIAN *(Greek)* Tame
VARIATIONS: Dameon, Damien, Damion, Damon, Daymon, Daymond

**DANIEL** *(Hebrew)* God is my judge
VARIATIONS: Danek, Danil, Danilo, Danko, Danniel, Dannson
NICKNAMES: Dan, Dana, Danny, Dhani

**DANTE** *(Spanish, Italian, Latin)* Enduring
VARIATIONS: Dantae, Dantel, Daunte, Donte

**DARIN** *(Irish)* Great
VARIATIONS: Daren, Darren, Darrie, Daryn

**DARRYL** *(French)* Beloved
VARIATIONS: Darrel, Darrell, Darren, Darrol, Darrow, Darryll, Daryl
NICKNAME: Derry

**DAVID** *(Hebrew)* Cherished
VARIATIONS: Daveed, Davide, Davin, Davis, Davit, Davyd, Dawson
NICKNAMES: Dave, Davey, Davie, Davy

**DEAN** *(English)* Valley
VARIATIONS: Deane, Dene, Dennit
NICKNAMES: Dee, Deno, Dino

**DELANEY** *(Irish)* Challenging
VARIATIONS: Delaine, Delano, Delany
NICKNAME: Del

**DEMARCO** *(African-American)* Of Mark
VARIATIONS: D'Marcus, Damarcus, Demarcus, Demario, Demarkis, Demarkus

**DEMETRIUS** *(Greek)* One who loves the earth
VARIATIONS: Demetre, Demetri, Dimitri, Dmitri, Dmitrias
NICKNAME: Demmy

**DENNIS** *(Greek)* Follower of Dionysus, God of Wine
VARIATIONS: Denis, Dennes, Dennison, Dennys, Denys, Dion, Dionis
NICKNAME: Denny

**DENZIL** *(Celtic)* Stronghold
VARIATIONS: Denzall, Denzel, Denziel, Denzill, Denzyl

**DEREK** *(English)* Famous leader
VARIATIONS: Darrick, Dederick, Dekker, Dereck, Deric, Derick, Derik, Derreck, Derrek, Derrick, Derrik, Deryck, Deryk
NICKNAMES: Dirk, Durk, Rick, Ricky

DESHAWN *(African-American)* God is giving
VARIATIONS: D'Chaun, DaShaun, DaShawn,
DeSean, DeShaun, Deshaun

DESMOND *(Latin)* The universe and heavens
VARIATIONS: Demon, Desmund, Dezmond
NICKNAMES: Des, Desi, Dezi

DEVIN *(Celtic)* Poet
VARIATIONS: Deven, Devon
NICKNAME: Dev

DEXTER *(Latin)* Right-handed
NICKNAME: Dex

DILLAN *(Irish)* Loyal
VARIATIONS: Dillon, Dilon, Dilyn
NICKNAMES: Dil, Dill

DIMITRI *(Slavic)* Fertile
VARIATION: Dmitri

DIRK *(Danish)* Variant of Derek
VARIATIONS: Dierick, Dirck

DOMINIC *(English)* Of the Lord
VARIATIONS: Domek, Domenic, Domicio,
Domingo, Dominick
NICKNAMES: Dom, Don, Nic, Nick, Nik

**DONALD** *(Celtic)* Ruler of world
VARIATIONS: Donahue, Donner, Donovan, MacDonald
NICKNAMES: Don, Donnie, Donny

**DOUGLAS** *(Gaelic)* Dark water
VARIATIONS: Dougal, Douglass
NICKNAMES: Doogie, Doug, Dougie, Dougy, Duggie

**DOV** *(Hebrew)* Bear
VARIATION: Dove

**DRAKE** *(Greek)* Serpent

**DUNCAN** *(Scottish)* Dark-skinned warrior
NICKNAME: Dunc

**DUSTIN** *(German)* Brave
VARIATION: Dustyn
NICKNAME: Dusty

# E

**EARL** *(English)* Leader
VARIATIONS: Earle, Erl, Erle, Errol, Erryl

**EDGAR** *(English)* Successful spearman
VARIATIONS: Ed, Eddie, Edgard, Edgardo, Edgars

**EDMUND** *(English)* Wealthy guard
VARIATIONS: Eadmund, Eamon, Edmundo

**EDWARD** *(English)* Happy
VARIATIONS: Edison, Edouard, Edson, Eduard, Eduardo, Edvard, Edwin, Edwyn
NICKNAMES: Ed, Edd, Eddie, Eddy

**EDWIN** *(English)* Rich in friendship
VARIATIONS: Ed, Edwinn

**ELI** *(Hebrew)* Faithful man
VARIATIONS: El, Elie, Eloy, Ely

**ELIJAH** *(Hebrew)* The Lord is my God
VARIATIONS: Elias, Elison, Eliya, Eliyah, Elliot, Ellis, Elya
NICKNAMES: El, Eli, Els

**ELLERY** *(English)* Island of elder trees
VARIATION: Ellary
NICKNAME: Ell

**ELROY** *(Irish)* Red-haired youth;
*(French)* The king
VARIATIONS: Elric, Elrick

**ELVIS** *(Scandinavian)* Wise
VARIATIONS: El, Elvys

**EMANUEL** *(Hebrew)* God is with us
VARIATIONS: Emanuele, Emmanuel, Imanuel,
Manuel
NICKNAME: Manny

**EMERY** *(German)* Industrious leader
VARIATIONS: Amory, Emerick, Emericus, Emerson,
Emil, Emile, Emilio, Emmery, Emmet, Emmory,
Emory

**ENNIS** *(Gaelic)* Island
VARIATION: Enos

**ERIC** *(Scandinavian)* Ruler with honor
VARIATIONS: Erek, Erich, Erick, Erico, Erik
NICKNAMES: Richie, Rick

**ERNEST** *(Old English)* Sincere
VARIATIONS: Earnest, Ernesto, Ernst
NICKNAMES: Ern, Ernie, Erno

**ERROL** *(Scottish)* Scottish place
VARIATIONS: Erroll, Erryl

**ERWIN** *(English)* Friend
VARIATIONS: Erving, Erwyn, Erwynn, Irving, Irwin

**ETHAN** *(Hebrew)* Steady
VARIATION: Etan

**EUGENE** *(Greek)* Born to excellency
VARIATIONS: Eugenio, Eugenius
NICKNAME: Gene

**EVAN** *(Welsh)* God is good
VARIATIONS: Evander, Evann, Evans, Evin, Evon, Ewan, Ewen

**EVERETT** *(English)* Powerful
VARIATIONS: Eberhard, Eberhart, Ebert, Everard, Everart, Everet, Everhard, Everitt

# F

**FABIAN** *(Latin)* Bean grower
VARIATIONS: Fabiano, Fabien, Fabius, Fabiyan, Fabyan, Fabyen

**FAHIM** *(Hindu)* Intelligent

**FARIS** *(Arabic)* Knight

**FELIX** *(Latin)* Great happiness
VARIATIONS: Felicio, Felis

**FERDINAND** *(German)* Adventurer
VARIATIONS: Fernand, Fernando
NICKNAMES: Ferd, Ferdie

**FIELDING** *(English)* Field
VARIATIONS: Field, Fielder

**FINIAN** *(Irish)* Fair
VARIATIONS: Findlay, Finlay, Finley, Finnian, Fionan, Fionn
NICKNAME: Finn

**FLOYD** *(Welsh)* Gray-haired

**FLYNN** *(Irish)* Red-haired man's son
VARIATIONS: Flin, Flinn, Flyn

**FOREST** *(French)* Woods
VARIATIONS: Forester, Forrest, Forrester, Forster, Foster

**FRANCIS** *(Latin)* Free spirit, Frenchman
VARIATIONS: Franchot, Francisco, Franco, François
NICKNAMES: Frank, Frankie

**FRASER** *(English)* Town in France
VARIATIONS: Frasier, Frazer, Frazier

**FREDERICK** *(German)* Peaceful leader
VARIATIONS: Frederic, Frederich, Frederico, Frederigo, Frederik, Fredric, Fredrick, Friedrich
NICKNAMES: Fred, Freddie, Freddy, Fritz

**FULLER** *(English)* One who shrinks and thickens cloth

**FULTON** *(English)* Field by the town

# G

**GABRIEL** *(Hebrew)* Man of God
VARIATIONS: Gabrielli, Gabriello, Gabris, Gavriel
NICKNAMES: Gab, Gabby

**GAINES** *(French)* To obtain
VARIATION: Gaynes

**GALLAGHER** *(Celtic)* Helper
NICKNAME: Gale

**GARDINER** *(Latin)* Enclosed garden
VARIATIONS: Gardener, Gardnard, Gardner

**GARETH** *(Welsh)* Gentle
VARIATIONS: Garith, Garret, Garreth, Garrett, Garyth
NICKNAMES: Garry, Gary

**GARRISON** *(French)* To protect
VARIATION: Garson
NICKNAMES: Garry, Garrey, Gary

GARY *(English)* Strong man
VARIATIONS: Garey, Garrey, Garri, Garry

GAVIN *(Welsh)* Hawk of the plain
VARIATIONS: Gauvin, Gavan, Gaven, Gavyn
NICKNAMES: Vin, Vinnie, Vinny

GENE *(Greek)* Well-born; short form of Eugene
VARIATIONS: Genio, Geno, Jeno

GEOFFREY *(German)* Peace
VARIATIONS: Godfrey, Gottfried, Jefferies, Jefferson, Jeffery, Jeffrey, Jeffries
NICKNAMES: Geoff, Jef, Jeff

GEORGE *(Greek)* Farmer
VARIATIONS: Georg, Georges, Georgi, Jorge

GERALD *(German)* Ruler with a spear
VARIATIONS: Geralde, Geraldo, Gerard, Geraud, Gerrald, Gerrold, Jerold, Jerrold
NICKNAMES: Gerry, Jerry

GILES *(English)* Bearer of shield
VARIATIONS: Gilles, Gyles
NICKNAME: Gil

GLEN *(Irish)* Narrow valley
VARIATION: Glenn

**GORDON** *(English)* Small, round hill
VARIATIONS: Gordan, Gorden
NICKNAMES: Gordie, Gordy

**GRADY** *(Latin)* Degree, grade

**GRAHAM** *(English)* Grand home
VARIATIONS: Graeham, Graeme, Grahame, Gram

**GRANGER** *(Latin)* Grain

**GRAYSON** *(English)* Son of the gray-haired man
VARIATIONS: Graydon, Greyson
NICKNAMES: Gray, Grey

**GREGORY** *(Greek)* Watchman
VARIATIONS: Gregor, Gregorio, Gregorius, Gregour
NICKNAMES: Greg, Gregg

**GRIFFIN** *(Latin)* Hooked nose
VARIATIONS: Griffith, Griffon, Gryphon
NICKNAME: Griff

**GUSTAVE** *(Scandinavian)* Staff of the Goths
VARIATIONS: Gustaf, Gustav, Gustavo, Gustavus
NICKNAME: Gus

**GUY** *(German)* Leader

# H

**HAKEEM** *(Arabic)* Brilliant
VARIATION: Hakim

**HALE** *(English)* Safe
VARIATIONS: Haley, Halford, Halley, Halset, Halsy,
Hollis
NICKNAME: Hal

**HAMID** *(Arabic)* Praised
VARIATIONS: Hammad, Hammed

**HAMILTON** *(English)* Castle
VARIATION: Hamelton
NICKNAME: Ham

**HANS** *(German)* German name for John
VARIATIONS: Handley, Hanes, Hanley, Hansel,
Hansen, Hanson, Haynes, Heinz, Honus

**HARLEY** *(German)* Field of hemp
VARIATIONS: Haldon, Halford,
Harald, Harlan, Harlen, Harlin,
Harlow, Hiraldo
NICKNAMES: Hal, Harry

**HAROLD** *(German)* Commander
VARIATIONS: Haldon, Halford, Harald, Harlow, Hiraldo
NICKNAMES: Hal, Harry

**HARRISON** *(English)* Harry's son
VARIATIONS: Harris, Harrisen
NICKNAME: Harry

**HART** *(English)* Mature male deer
VARIATIONS: Harte, Hartley, Hartwell, Heartley, Hersch, Herschel, Hersh, Hershel, Hertz, Hirsch, Hirsh

**HARVEY** *(French)* Worthy of battle
VARIATIONS: Harve, Harveson, Herve, Hervey
NICKNAME: Harv

**HAYDEN** *(English)* Hill of hay
VARIATIONS: Haddan, Haddon, Haden, Hadon, Hadyn, Haydn, Haydon, Hayes, Hayward, Haywood, Heywood

**HENRY** *(German)* Ruler
VARIATIONS: Enrico, Enrique, Hendrick, Henery, Henri, Henryk
NICKNAME: Hank

**HERBERT** *(German)* Shining soldier
VARIATIONS: Eberto, Herbertus, Heriberto
NICKNAMES: Herb, Herbie

**HERMAN** *(German)* Army man
VARIATIONS: Armand, Armando, Armant, Armin,
Harmon, Hermann, Hermon

**HILLEL** *(Hebrew)* Acclaimed

**HOLBROOK** *(English)* Brook close to a hollow
VARIATIONS: Holbrooke, Holden

**HOMER** *(Greek)* Pledge
VARIATIONS: Homère, Homerus, Omero

**HOWARD** *(English)* Observer
NICKNAME: Howie

**HOYT** *(Irish)* Spirit

**HUBERT** *(German)* Bright or shining intellect
VARIATIONS: Hobart, Hubbard, Huberto,
Humberto
NICKNAMES: Bert, Hube, Hubie, Huey

**HUGH** *(German)* Intelligent and spirited
VARIATIONS: Hobard, Hobart, Hubbard, Hubbell,
Hubert, Huet, Hugo, Uberto
NICKNAME: Huey

**HUNTER** *(English)* To pursue
VARIATIONS: Huntington, Huntley
NICKNAMES: Hunt

**HUXLEY** *(English)* Meadow full of ash trees
VARIATIONS: Haskel, Haskell
NICKNAMES: Hux, Lee

# I

**IAN** *(Scottish)* God is kind
VARIATIONS: Ean, Iain

**INCENCIO** *(Spanish)* One who is white

**INGHAM** *(English)* Area in Britain
VARIATIONS: Ingmar, Ingram, Ingrim

**INNES** *(Gaelic)* Isolated
VARIATIONS: Innes, Innis

**IRA** *(Hebrew)* Observant one

**IRVING** *(Irish)* Handsome
VARIATIONS: Ervin, Irvin, Irvington
NICKNAMES: Erv, Irv

**ISAAC** *(Hebrew)* One who laughs
VARIATIONS: Isac, Isak, Issak, Itzik, Izak
NICKNAMES: Zack, Zak

**ISAIAH** *(Hebrew)* God helps me
VARIATIONS: Isa, Isia, Isiah, Issa, Issiah

**ISHMAEL** *(Hebrew)* God hears
VARIATIONS: Ismael, Ismail, Yishmael

**IVAN** *(Russian)* God is good
VARIATIONS: Evon, Ivanchik, Ivanek, Ivano, Yvan, Yvon

**IVES** *(English)* Yew wood
VARIATION: Yves

# J

**JACKSON** *(English)* Son of Jack
VARIATION: Jakson
NICKNAMES: Jack, Jackie

**JACOB** *(Hebrew)* Follower
VARIATIONS: Jacoby, Jakab, Jakob, Jakub
NICKNAMES: Jaco, Jacke, Jakie

**JAFAR** *(Hindu)* Small stream

**JAMES** *(English)* Substitute
VARIATIONS: Diego, Jacques, Jaime, Jameson, Jamieson, Jamison
NICKNAMES: Jamie, Jim, Jimmey, Jimmy

**JAMIL** *(Arabic)* Handsome
VARIATION: Jamal

**JARED** *(Hebrew)* Descendant
VARIATIONS: Jarad, Jarid, Jarod, Jarrad, Jarred, Jarret, Jarrett, Jered, Jerod, Jerrod, Jerryd

**JARETH** *(African-American)* Adventuresome
VARIATIONS: Jarreth, Jerth

**JASON** *(Greek)* Healer
VARIATIONS: Jacen, Jaeson, Jaison, Jasper, Jaycen, Jaysen, Jayson
NICKNAME: Jay

**JAY** *(Latin)* Blue jay
VARIATIONS: Jae, Jai

**JEDIDIAH** *(Hebrew)* God's beloved
NICKNAME: Jed

**JEFFREY** *(German)* Peace
VARIATIONS: Geoffrey, Geoffry, Jefferies, Jeffery, Jeffries, Jeffry
NICKNAME: Jeff

**JEREMIAH** *(Hebrew)* The Lord exalts
VARIATIONS: Geremia, Jem, Jereme, Jeremias, Jeremy, Jerry

**JEREMY** *(Hebrew)* God will uplift
VARIATIONS: Gerome, Jeramee, Jeramey, Jeramie, Jereme, Jeremey, Jerome, Jeromy
NICKNAME: Jerry

**JEROME** *(Greek)* Holy
VARIATIONS: Gerome, Geronimo, Hieronymus, Jeromo
NICKNAMES: Gerrie, Gerry, Jerry

**JERRELL** *(African-American)* Exciting
VARIATIONS: Gerrell, Jarell, Jarrel, Jarrell, Jerus
NICKNAME: Jerry

**JERRY** *(German)* Strong
VARIATIONS: Gerry, Gery, Jerre, Jerrey, Jerrie

**JESUS** *(Hebrew)* God is my salvation

**JETT** *(English)* Hard black gem
VARIATION: Jeth

**JOACHIM** *(Hebrew)* God will determine
VARIATIONS: Joaquim, Joaquin

**JOEL** *(Hebrew)* God is Lord

**JOHN** *(Hebrew)* God is good and merciful
VARIATIONS: Jackel, Johann, Jon, Jonathan, Juan
NICKNAMES: Johnnie, Johnny

**JONAH** *(Hebrew)* Dove
VARIATIONS: Jonas, Yonah

**JOSEPH** *(Hebrew)* God will multiply
VARIATIONS: Jose, Josef, Josephe
NICKNAMES: Joe, Joey

**JOSHUA** *(Hebrew)* God is my salvation
VARIATIONS: Josiah, Josias, Josua
NICKNAME: Josh

**JUDE** *(Hebrew)* Praise God
VARIATIONS: Judah, Judas, Judd, Judson

**JULIAN** *(Latin)* Fair complexion
VARIATIONS: Julien, Julio, Julion, Julius
NICKNAME: Jules

**JUSTIN** *(Latin)* Righteous
VARIATIONS: Justino, Justis, Justus

# K

**KADEEM** *(Arabic)* Servant
VARIATION: Kadem

**KAI** *(Hawaiian)* Sea
VARIATION: Kye

**KAREEM** *(Arabic)* Generous
VARIATIONS: Karim, Karime

**KATO** *(African)* Second of twins
VARIATION: Kito

**KEANE** *(English)* Brave
VARIATIONS: Kain, Kaine, Kayne, Kean, Keanu,
Keenan, Keene, Kene, Kienan

**KEANU** *(Hawaiian)* The breeze
VARIATION: Keahnu

**KEATON** *(English)* Hawk's nest
VARIATIONS: Keeton, Keyton

**KEEFE** *(Irish)* Enjoyment
VARIATIONS: Keefer, Kief, Kiefer

**KEEGAN** *(Irish)* Passionate
VARIATIONS: Kagen, Keagan, Keegen, Kegan

**KEENAN** *(Irish, Gaelic)* Ancient
VARIATIONS: Keen, Keenon, Kennan, Kienan

**KEITH** *(Scottish)* Forest

**KELVIN** *(English)* River man
VARIATIONS: Kelvan, Kelven

**KENDALL** *(English)* Ruler
VARIATIONS: Kendal, Kendell
NICKNAME: Ken

**KENNETH** *(Irish)* Handsome
VARIATION: Kennith
NICKNAMES: Ken, Kenny

**KENT** *(Welsh)* Bright white

**KESHON** *(African-American)* Sociable
VARIATIONS: KeSean, KeShon

**KEVIN** *(Irish)* Handsome
VARIATIONS: Kevan, Keven, Kevon, Kevyn
NICKNAME: Kev

**KIEFER** *(German)* Barrel maker
VARIATIONS: Keefer, Keifer

**KIERAN** *(Irish, Gaelic)* Dark
VARIATIONS: Keiran, Keiron, Keran, Kiernan, Kieron

**KIRBY** *(English)* Village of the church
VARIATIONS: Kerbey, Kerbie, Kirbey, Kirbie

**KIRK** *(Scandinavian)* Church

**KNOTON** *(Native American)* Wind

**KNOWLES** *(English)* Grassy hill
VARIATION: Nowles

**KNOX** *(English)* Hills

**KOBE** *(African)* Tortoise

**KWAME** *(Ghanaian)* Saturday's child
VARIATIONS: Kwamee, Kwami

**KYLE** *(Gaelic)* Narrow, straight
VARIATIONS: Kile, Kiley, Kye, Kylan, Kylen, Kyler,
Kyrell

# L

**LAMONT** *(French)* The mountain
VARIATIONS: Lammond, Lamond, LaMond, Lemont
NICKNAME: Monty

**LANCELOT** *(Latin)* Sharp spear
VARIATIONS: Lancin, Lansing
NICKNAME: Lance

**LANDAN** *(German)* Open space
VARIATIONS: Lander, Landers, Landis, Landon

**LANGSTON** *(English)* Long town

**LAVONN** *(African-American)* Small one
VARIATIONS: LaVaun, LaVoun

**LAWRENCE** *(English)* Crowned with a laurel
VARIATIONS: Laurance, Laurence, Lawrance, Loren, Lorence, Lorens, Lorentz, Lorenz, Lorenzo, Loring
NICKNAME: Larry

LAWSON *(English)* Son of Lawrence
VARIATIONS: Laughton, Lawford, Lawton

LEELAND *(English)* Shelter
VARIATIONS: Leighland, Leland
NICKNAME: Lee

LEIF *(Scandinavian)* Beloved
VARIATIONS: Leaf, Lief

LEITH *(Scottish, Gaelic)* Broad river

LENNOX *(Scottish)* Elm trees
VARIATION: Lenox
NICKNAMES: Len, Lenny

LEO *(Greek)* Lion, strength
VARIATIONS: Leon, Leopold, Lionel, Lon, Lyons,
Lyonel

LEONARD *(German)* Bold as a lion
VARIATIONS: Lenard, Lennard, Leonardo, Linek,
Lon
NICKNAMES: Len, Lennie, Lenny, Lonnie, Lonny

LEROY *(French)* King
VARIATIONS: LeeRoy, LeRoi, LeRoy
NICKNAME: Lee

LESTER *(Latin)* From the camp or legion
NICKNAME: Les

**LEVI** *(Hebrew)* Harmonious
VARIATIONS: Levey, Levy
NICKNAME: Lev

**LEYLAND** *(English)* Uncultivated land

**LIAM** *(Irish)* To protect
VARIATIONS: Lian, Lyam

**LINUS** *(Greek)* Flaxen-haired
VARIATIONS: Lino, Linos

**LLOYD** *(Welsh)* Sacred
VARIATION: Loyd

**LOGAN** *(Irish)* Hollow or cove

**LOUIS** *(French)* Warrior
VARIATION: Lewis
NICKNAMES: Lew, Lou

**LOWELL** *(English)* Wolf
VARIATION: Lowel

**LUCAS** *(English)* Area in Italy
VARIATIONS: Lucius, Lukas
NICKNAMES: Luc, Luke

**LUKE** *(Greek)* Illuminating
VARIATIONS: Lucas, Lukas
NICKNAMES: Luc, Luck, Lucky

**LYLE** *(French)* Island
VARIATIONS: Lisle, Lyall, Lyell, Lysle
NICKNAME: Ly

**LYNDON** *(Old English)* Linden tree hill
VARIATIONS: Linden, Lindon, Lyndell, Lynden
NICKNAMES: Lin, Lindy, Lyn

# M

**MAC** *(Scottish)* Son
VARIATION: Mack

**MACAULAY** *(Scottish)* Son of the moral one
NICKNAME: Mac

**MACON** *(English)* To create

**MADDOX** *(Welsh)* Generous
VARIATIONS: Maddoc, Maddock, Madoc, Madoch, Madock, Madox

**MADU** *(African)* People

**MAGUIRE** *(Irish)* Subtle
VARIATIONS: MacGuire, McGuire, McGwire

**MAKOTO** *(Japanese)* Honesty

**MALACHAI** *(Hebrew)* Angel
VARIATIONS: Malachi, Malachy
NICKNAME: Mal

**MALCOLM** *(English)* Servant
VARIATIONS: Malcolum, Malcom, Malkolm, Maolcolm
NICKNAME: Mal

**MALIK** *(Arabic)* Sovereign
VARIATIONS: Maleek, Malek, Mallik

**MANNING** *(English)* To care for
VARIATION: Manville
NICKNAME: Manny

**MARIANO** *(Spanish, Latin)* Manly
VARIATION: Mario

**MARK** *(Latin)* To shine
VARIATIONS: Marc, Marceau, Marcel, Marcello, Marco, Marcos, Marcus, Marek, Mario, Marius, Markos, Markus

**MARSHALL** *(French)* High office
VARIATIONS: Marschal, Marshal
NICKNAME: Marsh

**MARTIN** *(Latin)* Warlike
VARIATIONS: Martan, Martel, Marten, Martino, Martinos, Martins, Marton, Martyn
NICKNAME: Marty

**MASON** *(French)* Stone worker
VARIATION: Masson
NICKNAME: Mace

**MATTHEW** *(Hebrew)* Gift of God
VARIATIONS: Mateo, Mateus, Mathew, Mathias, Mathieu, Matias, Matteo, Matthias, Mattias
NICKNAMES: Matt, Matty

**MAURICE** *(Latin)* Dark-skinned
VARIATIONS: Mauricio, Morice, Moriss, Morrice, Morris, Morriss
NICKNAMES: Maurie, Morry

**MAXIMILIAN** *(Latin)* Greatest
VARIATIONS: Massimo, Max, Maxim, Maximillian,
Maximo, Maximos, Maxwell
NICKNAME: Maxy

**MICHAEL** *(Hebrew)* Who is like God?
VARIATIONS: Maguel, Makis, Micah, Michail,
Michal, Michel, Miguel, Mikael, Mikel, Mikhail,
Mikhos, Mikkel, Mikko, Misha
NICKNAMES: Mike, Mikey

**MILES** *(German)* Beloved, gentle
VARIATIONS: Milan, Milo, Myles

**MILTON** *(Old English)* Mill town
VARIATION: Millton
NICKNAMES: Milt, Miltie

**MITCHELL** *(Hebrew)* Variation of Michael, meaning "Who is like God?"
NICKNAME: Mitch

**MOHAMMED** *(Arabic)* Praised
VARIATIONS: Ahmad, Amad, Hamid, Hammad,
Hammed, Mohamad, Mohamed, Mohammad,
Muhammad

**MONROE** *(Scottish)* Turner
VARIATIONS: Monro, Munro, Munroe

MONTEL *(French)* Little mountain

MOSES *(Hebrew)* Saved from water
VARIATIONS: Moises, Mose, Mosha, Moshe, Mozes
NICKNAME: Moss

MURRAY *(Scottish)* Mariner
VARIATIONS: Moray, Murrey, Murry

# N

NABIL *(Arabic)* Prince

NATHANIEL *(Hebrew)* Gift of God
VARIATIONS: Nataniel, Nathan, Nathanael, Nathon
NICKNAME: Nat

NEIL *(Irish)* Champion
VARIATIONS: Neal, Neale, Neall, Neill, Neils,
Neilson, Nels, Nelson, Niels, Niles, Nilson

**NELSON** *(English)* Son of Neil
VARIATIONS: Nealson, Neils, Nils, Nilson, Nilsson

**NICHOLAS** *(Greek)* Victory
VARIATIONS: Niccolo, Nichol, Nicolas, Nicolaus, Nicolo, Niklos, Nikolai, Nikolais, Nikolas, Nikolaus, Nikolos, Nikos
NICKNAMES: Nick, Nicky

**NIGEL** *(Irish)* Champion
VARIATIONS: Nigal, Nigiel, Nigil

**NILES** *(English)* Smooth
VARIATIONS: Nile, Nyles
NICKNAME: Ni

**NOAH** *(Hebrew)* Long-lived
VARIATIONS: Noach, Noak

**NOLAN** *(Irish)* Proud one
VARIATIONS: Noland, Nolen, Nolin, Nollan

**NORMAN** *(English)* Northerner
VARIATIONS: Normand, Normando, Normann, Norris
NICKNAMES: Norm, Normie

**NURI** *(Arabic)* Light
VARIATIONS: Noori, Nuri, Nuriel, Nury

**OBI** *(African)* Heart

**OGDEN** *(English)* Oak tree valley
VARIATIONS: Ogdan, Ogdon

**OLAF** *(Scandinavian)* Ancestor

**OLIVER** *(Latin)* Olive tree
VARIATIONS: Olivier, Olivor, Ollivor
NICKNAMES: Olley, Olllie

**OMAR** *(Arabic)* Long life
VARIATIONS: Omarr, Omer, Omri

**ORLANDO** *(Italian)* Renowned throughout the land
VARIATIONS: Arland, Arlando, Arlo, Orim, Orland, Orleans, Orlo, Orval, Orville

ORSON *(Latin)* Bear
VARIATION: Urson
NICKNAME: Sonny

OSCAR *(English)* Divine spear
VARIATIONS: Oskar, Osker
NICKNAME: Ossie

OTIS *(Old English)* Son of Otto
VARIATIONS: Oates, Otess

OWEN *(Welsh)* Well born
VARIATIONS: Owain, Owayne, Owin

OZ *(Hebrew)* Strength
VARIATION: Osmand
NICKNAMES: Ozzie, Ozzy

# P

**PACO** *(Native American)* Eagle

**PARKER** *(English)* Park attendant
VARIATIONS: Park, Parke, Parkes, Parks

**PATRICK** *(Irish)* Noble
VARIATIONS: Patek, Paton, Patric, Paxton, Payton, Peyton
NICKNAMES: Paddie, Paddy, Pat

**PAUL** *(Latin)* Small
VARIATIONS: Pablo, Paolo, Paulino, Paulos, Pavel, Pavlo, Powel, Powle
NICKNAME: Paulie

**PENN** *(Latin)* Quill pen, writer

**PERRY** *(Latin)* Wanderer
VARIATIONS: Parry, Perrie

**PETER** *(Greek)* Rock
VARIATIONS: Pearce, Pearson, Pearsson, Pedro, Peers, Peeter, Peirce, Petko, Petras, Petro, Petronio, Petros, Pier, Pierce, Pierre, Pierrot, Pierrson, Piers, Pierson, Piet, Pieter, Pietrik, Pietro
NICKNAMES: Peat, Pete, Petey

# Who is Natalie Renee McIntyre?

*We've all heard that Marilyn Monroe's real name was Norma Jean Baker and Muhammad Ali started life as Cassius Clay. Even some of today's younger stars are finding reasons for using an assumed name. Here are a few of your favorites.*

Jennifer Aniston: *Jennifer Anastassakis*

Marc Anthony: *Marco Antonio Muniz*

Nicolas Cage: *Nicolas Coppola*

Tom Cruise: *Thomas Cruise Mapother IV*

Vin Diesel: *Mark Vincent*

Jamie Foxx: *Eric Bishop*

Macy Gray: *Natalie Renee McIntyre*

Faith Hill: *Audrey Faith Perry*

Alicia Keys: *Alicia Augello Cook*

Chaka Khan: *Yvette Marie Stevens*

Courtney Love: *Love Michelle Harrison*

Demi Moore: *Demetria Gene Guynes*

Brad Pitt: *William Bradley Pitt*

Charlie Sheen: *Carlos Irwin Estevez*

Bruce Willis: *Walter Bruce Willis*

Tiger Woods: *Eldrick Woods*

**PHILIP** *(Greek)* Lover of horses
VARIATIONS: Felipe, Felipino, Filip, Filipo, Filippo, Fillipp, Phillie, Phillios, Phillip, Phillipe, Phillipp, Phillippe, Phillips
NICKNAMES: Phil, Pip

**PHINEAS** *(Hebrew)* Oracle
VARIATIONS: Pinchas, Pinchos

**PHOENIX** *(Greek)* Everlasting

**PIERCE** *(Greek)* Rock
VARIATIONS: Pearson, Piers, Pierson

**PORTER** *(Latin)* Gatekeeper

**POWELL** *(English)* Son of Howell
VARIATION: Powel

**PRESCOTT** *(English)* Priest's cottage
VARIATIONS: Prescot, Prestcot, Preston

**PRICE** *(Welsh)* Vigorous
VARIATION: Pryce

# Q

**QUENTIN** *(Latin)* Fifth
VARIATIONS: Quenten, Quenton, Quintin, Quinton
NICKNAME: Quint

**QUINCY** *(French)* Estate of the fifth son
VARIATION: Quincey
NICKNAMES: Quince, Quinn

**QUINLAN** *(Irish)* Strong man
VARIATIONS: Quinlen, Quinley, Quinlin, Quinly
NICKNAME: Quinn

# R

**RAFI** *(Arabic)* Exalted
VARIATIONS: Rafe, Rafferty, Raffi

**RALPH** *(English)* Fearless counselor
VARIATIONS: Ralf, Ralston, Rauf, Rauffe

**RANDOLPH** *(English)* Wolf that protects

VARIATIONS: Randal, Randall, Randell, Randolf, Raoul

NICKNAMES: Randie, Randy

**RAPHAEL** *(Hebrew)* God has healed

VARIATIONS: Rafael, Rafel, Rafello, Raffaello

NICKNAMES: Rafi, Raphi

**RASHID** *(Turkish)* Righteous

VARIATIONS: Rasheed, Rasheid, Rasheyd

**RAVI** *(Sanskrit)* Sun god

VARIATION: Ravee

**RAYMOND** *(German)* Advisor

VARIATIONS: Raimondo, Raimund, Raimunde, Raimundo, Ramon, Ramond, Ramund, Raymund, Raymunde, Raymundo, Reimond

NICKNAME: Ray

**REGINALD** *(Latin)* Ruler's advisor

VARIATIONS: Reginalt, Reginauld, Reginault, Regnault, Reinald, Reinaldo, Reinaldos, Reinhold, Renaud, Renault, Ronald

NICKNAMES: Reg, Reggie,

**REGIS** *(Latin)* Kingly

**REUBEN** *(Hebrew)* Behold a son
VARIATIONS: Reubin, Ruben, Rubin
NICKNAME: Rube

**REX** *(Latin)* King, ruler

**RICHARD** *(German)* Powerful ruler
VARIATIONS: Ricard, Ricardo, Riccardo, Richardo, Richardon, Rickard, Rico, Riocard, Ritchard, Ritcherd
NICKNAMES: Dick, Ric, Rick, Rickey, Ricky

**ROBERT** *(English)* Renowned and bright
VARIATIONS: Robard, Robart, Robbin, Robers, Roberto, Roberts, Robertson, Robin, Robinson, Robson, Ruberto, Rupert, Ruperto
NICKNAMES: Bob, Bobbey, Bobbie, Bobby, Rip, Rob, Robb, Robbi, Robbie, Robby, Robi, Rori, Rory, Roy

**RODNEY** *(English)* Island of reeds
VARIATIONS: Roderic, Roderich, Roderick, Roderigo, Rodnee, Rodnie, Rodny, Rodrique
NICKNAMES: Rod, Rodd, Roddie, Roddy, Rori, Rory

**ROGER** *(German)* Renowned warrior
VARIATIONS: Rodger, Rodgers, Rogerio, Rogers, Ruggerio, Ruggero, Rutger, Ruttger
NICKNAME: Rog

**ROMAN** *(Latin)* From Rome
VARIATIONS: Romain, Romano, Romanos, Romeo, Romulo, Romulos, Romulus

**RONALD** *(English)* Powerful advisor
VARIATIONS: Ranald, Renald, Roald, Ronello, Roone
NICKNAMES: Ron, Ronn, Ronney, Ronni, Ronnie, Ronny

**ROSS** *(Scottish)* Cape
VARIATIONS: Rosse, Roswell, Russel, Russell
NICKNAMES: Rus, Russ

**ROWAN** *(Irish)* Red
VARIATIONS: Rooney, Rowen, Rowland, Rowney
NICKNAMES: Ro, Row

**ROWLAND** *(English)* Rugged terrain

**ROY** *(Irish)* Red
VARIATIONS: Roi, Royal, Royle, Royston

**RUDOLPH** *(Old German)* Famous wolf
VARIATIONS: Rodolf, Rodolph, Rudolfo, Rudolpho,
NICKNAMES: Rolf, Rudi, Rudie, Rudy

**RUSSELL** *(French)* Redhead
VARIATIONS: Russ, Russel

**RYAN** *(Gaelic)* Little king
VARIATIONS: Ryen, Ryon, Ryun

# S

**SAEED** *(African)* Happy

**SAMUEL** *(Hebrew)* God hears
VARIATIONS: Samouel, Sampson, Samson, Samuele,
Samuello, Sansom, Sanson
NICKNAMES: Sam, Sammie, Sammy

**SANTIAGO** *(Spanish)* Saint James
VARIATIONS: Sandiago, Sandiego, Santeago,
Santiaco

**SAWYER** *(English)* Woodworker
VARIATIONS: Sawyere, Sayer, Sayers, Sayre, Sayres

**SCOTT** *(English)* From Scotland
VARIATIONS: Scot, Scotto
NICKNAMES: Scottie, Scotty

**SEAN** *(Irish)* God is graceful
VARIATIONS: Seann, Shaine, Shane, Shaughn, Shaun, Shawn, Shayn, Shayne

**SEBASTIAN** *(Greek)* Venerable
VARIATIONS: Bastian, Bastiano, Bastien, Sebastien

**SETH** *(Hebrew)* Appointed

**SHAQUILLE** *(Arabic)* Handsome

**SIMON** *(Hebrew)* He who listens
VARIATIONS: Silas, Simeon, Simion, Simms, Simpson, Sims, Symms, Symon
NICKNAMES: Si, Sy

**SOLOMON** *(Hebrew)* Peace
VARIATIONS: Salman, Salomon,
Solaman, Soloman
NICKNAMES: Sol, Sollie

**SPALDING** *(English)* Divided
meadow
VARIATION: Spaulding

**SPENCER** *(English)* Seller of household goods
VARIATION: Spenser
NICKNAMES: Spence, Spense

**STANLEY** *(Old English)* Stony meadow
VARIATIONS: Stanlea, Stanlee, Stanly
NICKNAME: Stan

**STEPHEN** *(Greek)* Crowned
VARIATIONS: Esteban, Estien, Estienne, Etiennes,
Stefan, Stefano, Steffan, Steffen, Stefos, Stepan,
Stephan, Stephanus, Stevan, Steven
NICKNAMES: Steve, Stevie, Stevy

**STEWART** *(English)* Steward
VARIATIONS: Steward, Stuart
NICKNAMES: Stew, Stu

**SYLVESTER** *(Latin)* Wooded
VARIATIONS: Silvester, Silvestre
NICKNAME: Sly

# T

**TANNER** *(English)* One who tans leather
VARIATION: Tannier
NICKNAMES: Tan, Tanny

**TARIQ** *(Arabic)* Conqueror
VARIATIONS: Tareek, Tarek, Tarik

**TATE** *(English)* Happy
VARIATIONS: Tait, Taitt, Tayte

**TERENCE** *(Latin)* Roman family name
VARIATIONS: Terrance, Terrence, Torrance, Torrence
NICKNAMES: Tel, Telly, Terry, Torrey, Tory

**TERRY** *(Old German)* Power of the tribe
VARIATIONS: Terrey, Terri, Terrie

**THEODORE** *(Greek)* A gift or blessing from God
VARIATIONS: Teodor, Teodoro, Thaddaus,
Thaddeus, Thadeus, Theodor, Theodoro
NICKNAMES: Tad, Tadd, Ted, Tedd, Teddie, Teddy,
Telly, Thad, Theo, Tod, Todd

**THOMAS** *(Aramaic)* Twin
VARIATIONS: Tamson, Thoma, Thompson, Thomson, Tomas, Tomaso, Tomasso, Tomaz, Tomsen, Tomson
NICKNAMES: Tam, Thom, Tom, Tomie, Tomm, Tommie, Tommy

**TIMOTHY** *(Greek)* Respecting God
VARIATIONS: Timmothy, Timothe, Timothee, Timothey, Tymmothy, Tymon, Tymothey, Tymothy
NICKNAMES: Tim, Timmie, Timmy

**TOBY** *(Hebrew)* Short form of Tobias; God is good
VARIATIONS: Tobe, Tobee, Tobey, Tobie

**TODD** *(English)* Fox, sly
VARIATION: Tod
NICKNAMES: Toddie, Toddy

**TOSHIRO** *(Japanese)* Talented, intelligent

**TRAVIS** *(French)* Crossroads
VARIATIONS: Traver, Travers, Trevor

**TRENT** *(Latin)* Rushing waters
VARIATIONS: Trenten, Trentin, Trenton

**TREVOR** *(Irish)* Wise
VARIATIONS: Trevar, Trever

**TREY** *(English)* Three, creative
VARIATIONS: Tracey, Tracy, Tray, Troy

**TUCKER** *(English)* Cloth finisher
NICKNAME: Tuck

**TYLER** *(English)* Tile maker
VARIATION: Tylar
NICKNAME: Ty

**TYRONE** *(Greek)* Absolute ruler
VARIATIONS: Tirone, Tyron
NICKNAME: Ty

# U

**UMBERTO** *(Italian)* Earthy color
VARIATIONS: Humbert, Humberto

**UPTON** *(English)* Upper town, village

**URI** *(Hebrew)* God's light
VARIATIONS: Uria, Uriah, Urias, Uriel
NICKNAMES: Uri, Urie

# V

**VANCE** *(English)* Land of swamps
VARIATION: Vancelo
NICKNAMES: Van, Vann

**VAUGHN** *(Celtic)* Small
VARIATION: Vaughan

**VERNON** *(Latin)* Blossoming youth
NICKNAMES: Vern, Verne

**VICTOR** *(Latin)* One who conquers
VARIATIONS: Victoir, Victorio, Viktor, Vito, Vitor,
Vittorio, Vittorios
NICKNAMES: Vic, Vick

**VINCENT** *(Latin)* To be victorious
VARIATIONS: Vincente, Vincenz, Vincenzio, Vincenzo
NICKNAMES: Vin, Vinn, Vinnie, Vinny

**VITO** *(Latin)* Lively
VARIATIONS: Vital, Vitale

# W

**WADE** *(English)* To cross a stream
VARIATION: Wadell

**WALKER** *(English)* A person who shrinks, thickens, and cleans cloth
VARIATIONS: Walden, Waldo
NICKNAME: Walk

**WALLACE** *(English)* Stranger
VARIATIONS: Wallas, Walsh, Welch, Welsh
NICKNAMES: Wallie, Wally

**WALTER** *(German)* Ruler of the folk people
VARIATIONS: Walden, Waldo, Waldon, Walton
NICKNAMES: Wallie, Wally, Walt

**WARD** *(English)* To guard
VARIATIONS: Warde, Warden, Worden

**WAYNE** *(English)* Maker of wagons and wheels
VARIATIONS: Dwaine, Wain, Wainwright, Wayn,
Waynwright

**WESLEY** *(English)* Western grassland
VARIATIONS: Wellesley, Westbrook, Westcott,
Westin, Westleigh, Westley, Weston
NICKNAMES: Wes, West

**WHITFIELD** *(English)* Little field
VARIATIONS: Wheatley, Whitcomb, Whitley,
Whitney, Whittaker
NICKNAMES: Whit, Witt

**WILLIAM** *(German)* Determined protector
VARIATIONS: Vilem, Viliam, Wilem, Wilhelm,
Willard, Willem, Williamson, Willis, Willmer,
Wilmar, Wilmer, Wilmot, Wilson
NICKNAMES: Bill, Billie, Billy, Will, Willie, Willy

**WINSTON** *(English)* Victorious village
VARIATIONS: Winfield, Wingate, Winslow, Winthrop, Winton
NICKNAMES: Win, Winnie

**WYATT** *(French)* Little warrior
VARIATIONS: Wiatt, Wyat, Wyeth, Wyman

# X

**XAVIAR** *(Arabic)* Bright
VARIATIONS: Javier, Xavier

**XENOS** *(Greek)* Guest, stranger
VARIATIONS: Xeno, Zenos

# Y

**YALE** *(English)* On a high slope

**YARDLEY** *(English)* Enclosure
VARIATIONS: Yardlee, Yardleigh, Yardly
NICKNAMES: Lee, Leigh, Yard

**YASAHIRO** *(Japanese)* Serene

**YORK** *(English)* Estate of yew trees
VARIATIONS: Yorick, Yorke, Yorrick

**YOSHI** *(Japanese)* Quiet
NICKNAME: Yosh

**YUMA** *(Native American)* Son of the chief

**YVES** *(French)* Yew wood archer
VARIATION: Yvon

# Z

**ZACHARY** *(Hebrew)* Remembers God
VARIATIONS: Zacaria, Zacarias, Zacharia, Zachariah,
Zacharias, Zacharie, Zacherias, Zachery, Zackariah,
Zackery, Zakarias, Zakarie
NICKNAMES: Zach, Zack, Zak, Zeke

**ZAHID** *(Arabic)* Strict, devout

**ZAHUR** *(Swahili)* Flower
VARIATION: Zahir

**ZANE** *(English)* A form of John, meaning "God has
been gracious"
VARIATIONS: Zain, Zayne

**ZEUS** *(Greek)* Brightness, living
VARIATIONS: Zenon, Zinon

# Unisex Names

*Always end the name of your child
with a vowel, so that when you yell,
the name will carry.*

BILL COSBY

Girl? Boy? Maybe you know, or maybe you want to be surprised. Luckily, any of these gender-free names will be a perfect match.

You may have noticed the use of unisex names is on the rise. Although it's a new trend from the recent past, genderless names were also used in medieval England, when parents named children for saints. Saint or not, let's hope your little one will be as adaptable as his/her name!

# A

**ADRIAN** *(Greek)* Rich; *(Latin)* Dark, mysterious
VARIATIONS: Adrean, Adren, Adriana, Adriane, Adrianna, Adrianne, Adrienne
NICKNAMES: Addie, Addy

**AIDAN** *(Irish)* Warm

**ARIEL** *(Hebrew)* Spirited lion of God
VARIATIONS: Ari, Arie, Ariele, Arielle

**ASA** *(Hebrew)* Doctor

**AUBREY** *(German)* Powerful

**AVERY** *(English)* Wise ruler

# B

**BAILEY** *(English)* Bailiff, castle's outer wall
VARIATIONS: Baily, Baylee, Bayley, Baylie

**BANJI** *(African)* Second born of twins

**BLAIR** *(English)* Flat field
VARIATIONS: Blaire, Blayre

**146**

BLAISE *(English)* Torch
VARIATION: Blaze

BLAKE *(English)* Light or dark
VARIATIONS: Blaike, Blayke

BREESON *(American)* Powerful
VARIATIONS: Bree, Breece, Breese, Breson

BRETT *(French)* A person from Brittany
VARIATIONS: Brit, Britton

BROOKE *(English)* Small stream
VARIATION: Brook

# C

CAIRO *(African)* City in Egypt, confident
VARIATION: Kairo

CAMERON *(Celtic)* Bent nose

CAMPBELL *(Latin)* Open flat field

CAROL *(French)* Celebration in song
VARIATIONS: Carel, Carey, Carrol, Carroll, Caryl,
Karel, Sheryl

**CARY** *(Celtic, Gaelic)* Pure
VARIATIONS: Carey, Carrie

**CASEY** *(Irish, Celtic)* Brave, Observant
VARIATIONS: Casie, Cassidy, Kasey, Kasie
NICKNAME: Cass

**CODY** *(English)* Cushion
VARIATIONS: Codey, Codie, Coty, Kody

**CONNOR** *(Irish)* Much desire
VARIATIONS: Conner, Conor

**COREY** *(Irish)* The hollow
VARIATIONS: Correy, Cory

# D

**DAKOTA** *(Native American)* Tribal name, solid friend

**DALLAS** *(Scottish)* Town name, also means "wise"

**DANA** *(English)* From Denmark
VARIATIONS: Daina, Dane, Danna, Dayna

**DEVON** *(English)* Region in England, poetic

**DORSEY** *(Celtic)* From Dorset, meaning "people near the sea"

# If You've Got the Place, I've Got the Name

*Names taken from well-known cities, states and countries are all the rage these days. Perhaps a certain place has a special meaning for you. Here are some samples of fun "place" names for your newborn son or daughter:*

| | |
|---|---|
| Dakota | Madison |
| Dallas | Nevada |
| Denver | Paris |
| Florida | Phoenix |
| Georgia | Raleigh |
| Houston | Rochester |
| Indiana | Tennessee |
| Israel | Troy |

**DREW** *(English)* Wise one
VARIATIONS: Drewe, Dru

**DYLAN** *(Welsh)* Of the ocean
VARIATIONS: Dillan, Dillon

# E

**ESPEN** *(Scandinavian)* God bear

# F

**FLANNERY** *(Irish)* Red hair

**FRANKIE** *(Latin)* One from France

# G

**GARNET** *(Latin)* Deep red seed
VARIATIONS: Garner, Garnett, Grania

# H

HARPER *(English)* Harpist

HONOR *(Latin)* Acknowledgment

# I

ISRA *(Turkish)* Freedom, liberty

# J

JAIME *(English)* One who replaces
VARIATIONS: Jaimie, Jamie

JAYLIN *(American)* Possibly from Galen, meaning "calm"
VARIATION: Jalen

JESSE *(Hebrew)* Wealthy
VARIATIONS: Jessey, Jessie, Jessy
NICKNAME: Jess

**JORDAN** *(Hebrew)* To descend
VARIATION: Jorden
NICKNAME: Jordy

# K

**KANE** *(Welsh)* Beautiful
VARIATIONS: Kain, Kaine, Kayne, Keanu

**KEELY** *(Irish)* Attractive
VARIATIONS: Kealey, Kealy, Keeley, Keelie

**KELLY** *(Irish)* Lively, soldier
VARIATIONS: Keeley, Keely, Kelley, Kelli, Kellie
NICKNAME: Kell

**KELSY** *(English)* Island
VARIATION: Kelsey

**KERRY** *(Irish)* County in Ireland, dark-haired
VARIATIONS: Keri, Kerrey, Kerri, Kerrie

**KIRAL** *(Turkish)* Almighty chief

**KYLE** *(Scottish)* Narrow land
VARIATION: Kylie

# L

**LARUE** *(French)* The street

**LEE** *(English)* Meadow
VARIATION: Leigh

**LESLEY** *(Scottish)* Low meadow
VARIATIONS: Leslie, Lesly
NICKNAME: Les

# M

**MACKENZIE** *(Irish)* Child of wise leader
VARIATIONS: MacKenzie, McKenzie

**MADISON** *(English)* Of a good heart
VARIATIONS: Maddison, Madisson
NICKNAME: Maddy

**MAHARI** *(African)* Forgiver

**MARLON** *(French)* Wild falcon

**MORGAN** *(Welsh)* Brilliance

**MURPHY** *(Celtic)* High-spirited

# N

**NALIN** *(Hindi)* Lotus flower

**NALO** *(African)* Lovable

# O

**ORION** *(Latin)* Rising sun
VARIATIONS: Oren, Oriana

# P

**PALANI** *(Hawaiian)* Free man

**PALMER** *(English)* Carrying palm branches
VARIATIONS: Pallmer, Palmar

**PEYTON** *(English)* Village of the soldier

**PILLAN** *(Native American)* Storm God

# Q

QIMAT *(Hindi)* Of value

QUENNELL *(French)* Oak tree

# R

READE *(English)* To advise
VARIATIONS: Read, Reid

REECE *(Welsh)* Rashness
VARIATIONS: Rees, Reese, Rhys

RENÉ *(French)* Reborn
VARIATIONS: Renata, Renay, Renée, Reney
NICKNAMES: Reni, Renie, Renni, Rennie, Renny

RILEY *(Irish)* Brave
VARIATIONS: Reilly, Ryley

RIVER *(French)* Stream
VARIATION: Rivers

ROBIN *(English)* Bright fame, robin bird
VARIATIONS: Robbin, Robbyn, Robyn

RUSTY *(French)* Red-haired
VARIATION: Rustie

# S

**SHAWN** *(Hebrew)* God is good
VARIATIONS: Sean, Seann, Shaine, Shane, Shaughn, Shaun, Shawn, Shayn, Shayne

**SHELLY** *(English)* Meadow on ledge
VARIATION: Shelley

**SKYLAR** *(Dutch)* Shelter
VARIATION: Schuyler
NICKNAME: Skye

**SLOANE** *(Celtic)* Powerful defender

**SOLARIS** *(Greek)* Relating to the sun

**STACEY** *(Greek)* Hopeful
VARIATIONS: Stacia, Stacie, Stacy

**SYDNEY** *(French)* Enthusiastic
VARIATIONS: Sidney, Sydnie
NICKNAMES: Sid, Syd

# Straight from the "Art"

*Will your baby boy or girl have an artistic nature? Giving your child the name of a great artist, writer, or composer could help bring out his or her muse. Be creative with names like:*

| | |
|---|---|
| Auden | Melville |
| Blake | Mozart *or* |
| Dante | Mozartiana |
| Dylan | Picasso |
| Eliot | Raphael *or* |
| Emerson | Raphaela |
| Eudora | Sylvia |
| Faulkner | Tennyson |
| Flannery | Twain |
| Kipling | Whitman |
| Langston | Yeats |
| Leonardo | Zora |

# T

**TAYLOR** *(English)* Tailor by occupation
VARIATIONS: Tailer, Tailor, Tayler, Tyler

**TRACY** *(English)* Brave
VARIATIONS: Trace, Tracey, Traci, Tracie

**TRISTAN** *(Celtic)* Bold, daring
VARIATION: Tristam

# U

**UMI** *(African)* Servant

# V

**VALENTINE** *(Latin)* Strong
VARIATIONS: Valentin, Valentino, Valentyn
NICKNAME: Val

# W

**WHITNEY** *(English)* Tiny field
VARIATIONS: Whitnee, Whitnie, Whittney

**WILEY** *(English)* From the willows

# X

**XING** *(Chinese)* Star

**XUAN** *(Vietnamese)* Spring

# Y

**YAEL** *(Hebrew)* God's strength

**YAVAR** *(Hindu)* Meaning unknown

# Z

**ZAIRE** *(African)* Country name, from Zaire

**ZHI** *(Chinese)* Wisdom, healing

# And the Winners Are...

*According to the Social Security Administration, the top baby names in the United States for the year 2004, updated in May of 2005, are . . .*

| BOYS | GIRLS |
| --- | --- |
| 1. Jacob | 1. Emily |
| 2. Michael | 2. Emma |
| 3. Joshua | 3. Madison |
| 4. Matthew | 4. Olivia |
| 5. Ethan | 5. Hannah |
| 6. Andrew | 6. Abigail |
| 7. Daniel | 7. Isabella |
| 8. William | 8. Ashley |
| 9. Joseph | 9. Samantha |
| 10. Christopher | 10. Elizabeth |